CASH RICH
TIME RICH

CASH RICH TIME RICH

How To Ditch Your Boss and Live Life On Your Terms

MANNI CHOPRA

RETHINK PRESS

First published in Great Britain 2015
by Rethink Press (www.rethinkpress.com)

CONTENTS

My Story

The fact that you've picked up this book means you would probably like to have more money and more time in your life. You value your time and would like to be in control. And you are able to relate to one or more of these scenarios:

- You are in a job that pays you for your time.
- You are in a business that relies on you.
- You want a better quality of lifestyle.
- You want more time with your friends, family and for your hobbies.
- You don't want to compromise on the quality of your life.
- You want to have freedom from the 9–5 routine and have more flexibility and choice.
- You want to be able to do what you want, when you want and on your terms.
- Personal and time freedom is as important to you as money.

I meet people who are desperately seeking a residual income to fund their lifestyle. And this lifestyle can vary: paying fees for private schools or university, to getting married, a special honeymoon, family holidays, unique experiences with family and friends, leaving a legacy, working fewer days (part-time), helping a charity, spending time with kids. They want to give up their job to do what they love or supplement their job income.

When I am asked what I do and I tell people I invest in property and earn my living from the rental income I generate I often get the response: 'Ooh, that's far too risky'. I have had this response from people in all walks of life, including my neighbours who are professional writers, friends, family members, business owners, housewives, medical professionals and self-employed professional people. In my view walking down the road and driving is more risky as you could lose your life. Do you agree?

Let's face it, what's the worst thing that can happen when you educate yourself and invest your money, taking calculated risks? At worst you will break even. How can that be more risky than potentially losing your life?

In my view it is far riskier to carry on with life as normal and not invest your time to assess your current and future plans. There is proof that 95% of sixty-five-year-olds in this country retire in debt. In real terms your savings are devaluing in the banks. The majority of UK banks are currently providing a meagre 1–2% per annum interest for your savings. Inflation is on average 2% per annum.

People don't trust financial institutions, pension funds and other corporates to grow their money. If you are over fifty-five years of age, withdrawing all your pension funds from 6 April 2015 without considering the implications on tax and long term retirement plans is risky. Trust is also a big problem in the property industry as we have all heard stories of companies who have promised big and then disappeared or under delivered, but then selling your time for money (doing a job) is risky. What if you lose your job or your health and you can't work anymore? Have you got a 'Plan B'? Earning money in exchange for your time is a great way to give you a head start in life in the short term, but there is little or no flexibility, which results in compromising on your quality of life in the long run. People are living from pay cheque to pay cheque and not planning for long term security, building wealth or creating a legacy. If Plan A fails there is no backup.

I would like to share with you my life journey so far with all its ups and downs and I hope you can relate to some of it. I was brought up as the eldest of four in a traditional Sikh family in Mumbai and pretty much lived a 'cotton wool' existence. I was living at home when I got introduced to Romey Chopra, a British born Indian. From meeting him on day one, I got married to him in a court of law on day four, which was a big shock to the system. Before I knew it I found myself at London Heathrow, excited and nervous at the same time and looking forward to my new life in the UK.

Although I was a graduate from India, my qualifications were not valid in the UK and I had to start from scratch. I got a part-time job in Debenhams to make some money and become independent. I also started a part-time degree in Business and IT at Brunel University; IT seemed to be the thing to do, and a friend of mine was doing it.

Half way through my degree I landed a good IT job and started to feel more settled. We were leading the Double Income No Kids (DINKs) lifestyle and were fairly comfortable.

My journey into property began when, like millions of ordinary couples in this country, we had our first child. That's when I felt a bomb had exploded in our lives. Not really, of course, but it felt like our lives had turned completely upside down. A couple of months into my maternity leave I realised that I needed to start thinking about going back to work as I could only take up to a maximum of six months, having worked for my employer for less than two years. We had to decide between me quitting my job, sacrificing my income and compromising on our quality of life, or keeping my job and sending my son to a nursery, which I was dead against, especially at his tender age of six months. I spent a lot of sleepless nights thinking about what to do.

Luckily for me my husband's aunt came to my rescue and agreed to pick up my son, Rohan, and my nanny from home at 10am every weekday, then I would pick him up from their home after work. She was a godsend, and to this day I feel indebted to her.

Once I went back to work the day to day stress of juggling the demands of a full-time job and raising a young family started to take its toll on me. I was getting frustrated from the guilt of leaving my son at home every day as well as the work pressures. My day would typically start at 6am and I would get home around 7pm after picking my son up, followed by his bath and bed routine. More than anything I was upset that I couldn't spend any quality time with Rohan, but at that point I felt I had to keep going.

I had somehow managed it for a year when I found out I was pregnant with our second child. Knowing that my maternity break was around the corner kept me positive, and this time around I had the opportunity of taking a whole year off work as I had been in my job longer than two years.

After I had my second baby I really enjoyed my time off work. During my maternity break we moved house when my daughter was only five weeks old; the excitement of the baby along with moving house was crazy hectic. I had also planned a trip to Mumbai to visit my mum, staying with her for nearly six months to help me escape the depressing winter months in the UK and attending two close family weddings. While in Mumbai, with my mum's help I decided to do a diamond trading course with a view to starting my own business when I got back to the UK. I had met a supplier who was willing to give me his jewellery on the basis that he would exchange any stock that didn't sell.

During my maternity break I started selling the jewellery from home to friends and family. I also participated in a wedding show at London Olympia, which went down well. The break was coming to an end and it was decision time all over again. I was faced with the dilemma of whether I should give up my job and focus on running the diamond business or go back to work. The jewellery business would have required a big cash injection for stock, a retail unit, staff, systems, etcetera, and because we had bought a house just a year ago we had used up a lot of our savings. I reluctantly decided to go back to work.

My giving up work altogether would have put all the pressure on my husband to meet the ever increasing demands of raising a young family, although the child care costs for both the kids would pretty much wipe out my salary. Another reason for going back to work was that otherwise I would have had to face the reality of being a full-time mum and housewife, which somehow at the time seemed brain dead and depressing.

I wish I could turn the clocks back. I think deep down I had insecurities about not being able to get back to work if I took a long career break. After all, I had worked so hard to get to the point in my career where I was project managing a team.

I employed a full-time nanny to look after the kids, who were three and one at the time. I was working all hours given and didn't spend enough quality time with my kids. As time went by I started to feel inadequate and unhappy with myself as I couldn't do justice to my roles of Mum, wife and employee due to the lack of flexibility and control. I had twenty-six days annual leave, which was not enough to see me through sick days and holidays, and I started to resent my life.

Time flew by, and before I knew it my kids were eight and six. They started to demand that I pick them up from school every day; they said all mummies did it so why couldn't I do the same? That killed me inside. I also noticed that my son was withdrawn and seemed to be affected by the lack of quality time with me. I felt torn apart.

Deep down I had a feeling of being stuck in a 'time for money' trap and I had no choices. I felt cheated by the system; having done things the 'right' way, I thought to myself, Is this it? I had friends who were full-time stay-home mums and looked perfectly happy with their simple lives. I envied them and secretly wished I could be happy with just looking after the kids and doing the housework. We could have compromised on the quality of our lifestyle, downsizing from a five-bedroom to a three- or four-bedroom house and moving the kids to a state school, but we didn't feel it was right as we wanted to give our kids the best start we could afford by sending them to an independent school. Also I knew I had to keep my mind stimulated or else I would go insane.

Ideally I wanted to be in a situation where I could replace my job income with income from a business. Having worked in the corporate IT sector from 1998–2009, I decided it was time to review options going forward. I didn't want to waste another decade of my life on the same salary, and more importantly I wanted to spend quality time with the kids and be there for them.

As part of the looking at options process we considered property as one of our potential lines of business. Our small property portfolio at the time consisted of a couple of single-let flats in London and a multi-let property, our previous home that we had lived in before moving to our new house in Buckinghamshire, which we rented out to three unrelated tenants. While reviewing our portfolio we found that all the properties had increased in value and had gained a substantial amount of equity which would allow us to refinance and buy additional properties.

My focus was to network, educate myself and get all the knowledge I needed. One networking event I attended was the National Achievers Congress (NAC) in 2010. Robert Kiyosaki was one of the speakers, and so was Tony Robbins. Tony Robbins is a motivational speaker and life coach dedicated to help people achieve their dreams. Robert is the author of a bestselling book *Rich Dad, Poor Dad*, which examines concepts such as selling our time for money and having tax deducted before we get our pay cheque versus running a business and deducting expenses before getting taxed. He also explains the contrasting mindsets between a rich dad (a friend's dad) and poor dad (his own dad), giving us both viewpoints, and why he chose starting a business and building assets over being an employee and selling his time for money.

I was totally sold on the idea of starting my own business and I was adamant I wanted to change my working life at this point. Finally I made a decision to become *financially free*, which in simple terms meant replacing my job income with *passive* (rental) *income* and building our family property business.

In 2010, after many deliberations and discussions with my husband, I took a sabbatical from work for a year. During this time I educated myself on various property strategies. Ideally I wanted to be in a situation that meant I had reached my target income and didn't need to go back to my job at the end of the sabbatical.

Very quickly I realised that buying houses and converting them into professional house shares was the way to go. All the property education I had done was more generic and I had used up all my education funds so I started to go to networking events and met people who had experience in converting a house into a multi-let house share, the technical term being

Houses of Multiple Occupation (HMOs). Back then it was basic information like the best location to buy, ideal tenant profile, number of let-able rooms required to break even and make a profit I needed to know. I needed to understand how best to calculate bills, work out how to manage energy consumption to maximise income, tenant finding, referencing, etcetera. I viewed tens of properties on a daily and weekly basis. At first I didn't know what exactly I was looking for, but with time I began to narrow down the area, number of rooms, ideal price bracket and was feeling a lot more confident of investing in my very first HMO.

I knew from day one that my rental properties would provide good quality accommodation to my tenants, even if it meant spending more money. I am truly passionate about giving professional people a good quality of accommodation for two reasons: firstly because in my previous life (in Mumbai) I had lived in a small converted one-bedroom flat (originally a large studio) with my parents, three siblings and a maid, and to top it all my dad had a home office among all the chaos. I longed to have my own space and share a room with my siblings – at the time a two-bedroom flat was considered a decent standard of living for the middle class. I know the pain of not living well, and I believe that we all deserve to live well. Secondly because I have been a professional I can relate to the fact that they generally work long hours and deserve to come back to nice, clean and good quality accommodation.

I will tell you more about this later.

Your Why

What is your 'Why'? Are you tired and frustrated with your job? Would you like more flexibility in your work life? Would you like a better work–life balance?

I believe time is more precious than money. You can always earn the money back you might have lost, but you certainly cannot get your *time* back. A lot of people have ended up working in a job that they don't enjoy. They are doing it as a means to an end: to pay the bills and fund their lifestyle.

In my experience we can achieve financial independence by buying or controlling assets. Properties are a good source of (rental) income and can be passive when fully managed by a third party. When you own a few of these assets, the income that you earn from them can replace the income from your job. Once this happens, you can give up your job, but your why needs to be strong, genuine and, quite frankly, desperate, because the property investing business is not easy.

You will need to maintain a steady stream of deals and funding. Two important skills required are raising money and finding deals that stack, which requires incredible perseverance, grit and determination. You should really want it badly, so much so that it is your only chance for happiness and peace moving forward.

This will give you the motivation to make the right choices for you. If you can relate to all this and are looking to achieve personal and financial freedom from the rat race, now is a good time to start.

What can more money provide you? Whether you want more cash flow for a better lifestyle, to replace your income, to have more fun, to pay school fees, how are you proposing to get it? However you decide to achieve your goals, you will need support, motivation, encouragement, guidance, inspiration and a plan, among other things. How better to get it than from someone who has been there, done that?

I didn't want to spend my life slogging from 9–5, stressed about getting a pay rise or impressing my manager. My why was my kids. I wanted to spend quality time with them, and more importantly be there for them when they needed me. I wanted to have the simple pleasures of life, like dropping them at and picking them up from school, watching their sport performances, being home when they are off sick, etc.

> *Since your outcomes are all a result of your moment-to-moment choices, you have incredible power to change your life by changing those choices. Step by step, day by day, your choices will shape your actions until they become habits, where practice makes them permanent.*
>
> **Darren Hardy, *The Compound Effect***

This struck a chord with me and made me realise the importance of the choices we make. It is so simple yet profound.

Once we become aware of the possible outcomes of the choices we make and consciously consider their potential impact, we notice the difference it makes to our life in the long run. When I realised how my choices have shaped my life, I decided to review them. It was time I chose my family over my job. I started to think of the right choices I needed to make to help me spend quality time with my family and earn a good living at the same time. And that's why I chose property.

I also chose not to work for someone who would dictate to me when I could or couldn't take holidays, or pick up my kids from school, or be around when they are poorly. It took me back to my own childhood days when I felt I didn't have a close connection with my mum because she was too busy trying to make ends meet. I was one of four kids and didn't get any one-to-one attention, and I was adamant that I didn't want to repeat history. I am now very involved in my kids' lives and I know what's going on day to day.

On reviewing my goals, I thought about what motivates me to grow as a person, engage in self- and spiritual-development and grow my wealth. I very quickly realised that my family unit and my children are my motivations to keep striving for more.

As a society we are made to feel that money is evil and that it is our greed that keeps us wanting more money. I strongly believe that money is not my main driving force, but what I can do with my money. However I do know that money can help me provide the best opportunities for my children in their education and general development. It can help me live a more enriched lifestyle, explore the world, go on exciting holidays and enjoy amazing experiences with my family and friends.

Abundance of money also allows me to reinvest it in my property business, in my self-development, explore and follow my life calling and coach and mentor others to achieve the same. We need to be secure and free from financial worries before we can follow our life calling.

Property has given me the opportunity to get out of the rat race to enjoy the freedom of time, choose my career and invest in me, the person. It has allowed me to be there for my two children as they are growing up, to go on the path of self-discovery, learn more about myself, what I enjoy, focus on my core values in life and self-development. In a nutshell, investing in property, and more specifically converting to professional house shares, has given me the ability to replace my job income by rental income in just over a year, and I would like to help others to be in the same position.

I realised that I was so busy in my 9–5 routine that I didn't really have the time to discover what I wanted out of life. I was an angry and bitter person as I felt I was not in control of my own time. I resented friends who were housewives only because I couldn't do the simple things in life like picking up my kids from school. Financial freedom has given me the joy of being my own boss, controlling my business, my destiny, etcetera. I have the time to learn and follow my dreams; to know what I like and don't like.

For example, I have discovered my contrarian nature and that I will not follow the crowd. And how I enjoy being a leader more than being a follower. I would have never known these things about myself had I not had the time to discover them.

More on my why:

- To be there for my children and experience life with them.
- To enjoy life to the fullest – exotic holidays, exciting experiences (for example Go Ape), restaurants, theatre, drama, dance with family and friends.
- To give opportunities and support to Rohan and Rhea in their careers and extra-curricular activities.
- To invest in my potential, enhance my talents and discover and follow my life calling.
- To help family members in need.

Enough said about my why. It's your turn now to write your reasons why you want financial security, independence and freedom.

Exercise 1: Write down three reasons why you want to become financially free.

Plan B

With the help of this real life case study I would like to highlight the importance of having a backup plan in place.

Friends of ours, Mr and Mrs S, are forty-eight and forty-five years of age respectively. They are very well to do and have a Double Income No Kids (DINKs) lifestyle. They go on two to three holidays a year, live in a beautiful large detached house with three dogs, drive a 4x4 each, shop at Waitrose – you get the picture. They are well established in the freelance business they run.

A couple of years ago Mrs S finds herself out of a contract. Mr S carries on and is doing very well in his line of work, so Mrs S decides to stay at home. All is going well until one day he too finds himself out of a contract. They have an unencumbered property (no mortgage), but no income coming in – they are asset rich and cash poor. They start to dip into their savings; they have led an extravagant lifestyle in the past and are finding it hard to adjust to a more humble way of life.

Let's turn this example around and assume that instead of paying off their mortgage they had invested some of their earnings in buy-to-let properties. Those assets would now be generating a second income, the pain of losing their primary income would be dramatically reduced and they would not be in such a compromising situation.

This situation could have been far worse if they'd had a family to support. We work all our waking hours to give our families a good standard of living, and it could all potentially be taken away if one or both parents were to lose their job or their business went into decline.

In today's economy with no job security this can happen to any one of us. We need to recognise that we can counteract such a situation by having a Plan B in place. If you invest your savings wisely you can build yourself a small property portfolio that consistently brings in secondary income on a monthly basis. This can be either reinvested or used to fund your and your family's lifestyles, be it school fees, more holidays, a new kitchen – what have you.

I believe that my three step API method can help you kick start your Plan B.

Step 1 – Analyse.
Step 2 – Plan.
Step 3 – Implement.

Step 1. Analyse. The first step is a fact-finding exercise. It is very important to know what you want to achieve. This means working out how much cash flow you need to generate per month to replace or supplement your income. For that you will need to work out your current monthly expenses.

This is an example of how it should look depending on your personal choices.

Plan A	Plan B
£2k a month	£3k a month
No time	working 3 days a week
One family dinner (eating out) a month	One family dinner (eating out) a week
Kids in state school	Kids in private school
A local holiday a year	An international holiday a year

Step 2. Plan. Your plan will have details about funding options available to you, be it savings, refinance money, Mum and Dad's bank or any other joint ventures you can do with family and/or friends.

Based on your access to funds, the plan will document the ideal property investment strategy, your goldmine area to invest, the number of properties you need to achieve your target, etcetera.

Please list all potential joint venture partners and collaborations.

Step 3. Implement. The implementation consists of putting the plan into action using my unique RICH formula (Section 4) which you can follow step-by-step. This approach will help you achieve your goals for personal freedom and financial abundance.

My vision is to help families experience true wealth through financial abundance. And I hope this book can guide and inspire you to get out of your comfort zone and follow your dreams in a systematic way through property investing.

Goals

Brian Tracy is a leading personal development guru who coaches people on time management, success, personal wealth, business, leadership and more. According to him, self-discipline is *the* most important habit for success. And goal writing is one such discipline.

To live the life you want, you must first understand and know exactly what things about your life you want to change. These generally tend to be in the areas of health (and fitness), wealth (job or business) and happiness (family, relationships – personal and spiritual).

Your goals need to be specific and articulated in words so they are crystal clear in your mind. Inspired by Brian Tracy, I have devised a simple proven three-step formula to help you achieve your goals.

1 – Think it.
2 – Ink it.
3 – Implement it.

Think it; To get empowered to pursue your goals you must visualise yourself having achieved those goals. For me a goal was to see myself in size 10 black skinny jeans, looking and feeling fabulous and in good shape.

Also feel the joyful abundance of what it would be like to achieve the end result. What would your family and friends be saying if you had reached your target?

Ink it; As Brian Tracy said, 'The daily practice of goal writing has changed the life of many'. Always write your goals in the present tense as though you have already achieved them.

The examples are below to help you word your goals correctly:

1   In October 2015 my property lettings and acquisition business is making £100,000 net income per annum.
2   In July 2015 I weigh 10 stone in weight and can fit into Zara size 10 black skinny jeans.
3   From January 2015 I meditate from 6.15–6.30am every morning.

Implement it; This involves writing down the action steps you would need to perform for you to meet your goals. Using one of the above examples I will illustrate how I plan to achieve a goal this year.

Goal: In October 2015 my property lettings and acquisition business is making £100,000 net income per annum.

Plan: I worked out how much more monthly income I need.

I produced a business growth plan and specified our sales target from existing services and potential new services we can introduce (inventory).

For each service we offer (example tenant finding) I took the following action steps:

1 Specify a monthly sales target and a plan of how we will achieve this.
2 Monitor actuals versus targets on a monthly basis.
3 Update plan as required.

As a result of this exercise my business had to be prepared to take on board additional costs like recruiting and training new staff, extra time, commission, etcetera.

Tracking your goals My suggestion is to choose three areas of your life that would be most positively impacted if you were to achieve the goals. Personally I have chosen health (and fitness), wealth (business) and happiness (spiritual and personal).

However, I have found one thing that lets most people down is the lack of momentum – implementation paralysis, you could say. Everyone is so busy making a living that they write their goals and do very little or nothing to move them closer.

I would like to share with you this one tool that has helped me tremendously, and I am sure it will help you too. It is something I have learned from Darren Hardy's book *The Compound Effect.*

It is as simple as tracking. For example, if you want to save more every month, you will need to have detailed knowledge of where and how your money is spent. You will need to keep a notepad and pen handy and log every penny you spend. Every time you buy online or at the supermarket, go to a restaurant, drink coffee, etcetera, you log it in your tracking notepad.

After just a week you will notice fascinating insights into your spending habits, and if you persevere for three weeks or more it will become a habit. Once you know where exactly you are spending your money you can then decide what to cut back on. This money can be placed in a 'peace of mind' account or invested.

You can use the same tool to achieve any of your goals.

What Is Financial Independence and Financial Freedom?

The two in my view are one and the same thing.

The Wikipedia definition of financial independence is as follows:

> *Financial independence is generally used to describe the state of having sufficient personal wealth to live, without having to work actively for basic necessities. For financially independent people, their assets generate income that is greater than their expenses.*

In my own words financial independence means creating different streams of passive income that meet your expenses and support your lifestyle. You can have a combination of one or more businesses, stocks and shares income, rental income from your property portfolio churning out x amount of money every month. This money not only pays your bills and supports your lifestyle, but you are also free to pursue other business and personal opportunities, be they hobbies or passions that you enjoy or becoming a philanthropist, etcetera.

In other words, you have the flexibility and choices to be, have and do what you want in life, being in a position to make a choice. Financial freedom/independence to me means that you are not exchanging your time for money. You don't have to go to work every day. You are the master of your own time and can spend it as per your goals.

In addition to financial freedom you also have time freedom, and freedom of choosing whom you work with and spend your time with as opposed to having to be at work with colleagues you may or may not get on with.

I would like to continue to share with you my personal journey to financial independence started in Section 1.

Sabbatical and trials and tribulation, 2010–2011

I had come to the conclusion that I would need to leave my job to pursue my dreams of being financially free. My husband, being self-employed, feared the worst and thought my taking a sabbatical would be a safer option. Secretly I was planning to achieve my goal within this period so I didn't have to go back to work. I had set myself a tough challenge, although at the time I was really blasé about it, thinking how difficult can it be?

In my mind I had planned how I would get the funding, I just needed to convince my husband it was the right thing to do. I was going to fund my first purchase by re-mortgaging one of my properties in London. I knew it had gone up in value and had a fair amount of equity that I could withdraw.

For my second property I was going to use the profit I had made by investing in a new build two-bedroom apartment in South Mumbai. When I first bought the property in Mumbai in 2004 the market was stagnant, and luckily for us the market had taken off at that point and the property prices sky rocketed.

During the sabbatical I invested my time in a few property educational courses that taught me all I needed to know about investing strategies, formulas to calculate yield, ROI (return on investment), net income and all the financial and technical aspects. After these courses I felt empowered, but also overwhelmed, not entirely clear in my mind about the best options to follow. Looking back I realise I had been tempted by the claims a lot of property courses make that it is easy to invest in property, and you don't need money, you can buy property for a £1, blah, blah, blah. I got carried away and a bit greedy and wanted everything for nothing, so I wasted time pursuing these strategies only to realise that I needed to do what I had done in the past, which is to recycle my cash and invest using these funds. Technically I haven't used my own money even though I am paying interest on the higher amount of loan (re-mortgage) I have taken from the lenders.

Eventually it became clear to me that I wanted to invest in the multi-let strategy. Once my strategy was clear I started to attend networking events, speaking to experienced landlords, listening to hundreds of webinars. I was totally immersed in property and loved learning.

Having already spent a lot of money on courses, I realised that I had a lot of knowledge about general strategies, but not enough depth for my strategy. Basic information that I now regard as common knowledge, like optimum number of rooms, monthly bills cost, furniture pack costings, refurbishment estimates, I did struggle with. When looking at a property with damp issues, roof problems, rising damp and other such technical issues, or recognising subsidence in a property, I did not know the cost for remedial work.

Typically I would view thirty to forty properties in a week and make lots of offers, mostly below market value (BMV) and I would lose out to higher bidders. One tip I can now pass on to save you grief is don't necessarily offer BMV. If you can make the numbers work at market price you will be in a stronger position to secure the deal. This obsession alone cost me a few months' delay in getting my first deal.

My husband also had very strict criteria and would reject most deals I brought to the table. This was very frustrating and it created tension in our relationship; I took it as a personal insult every time he rejected a deal I thought was good. I felt the pressure and the clock was ticking for me.

After six months of long working days, hundreds of viewings, lots of ground work, analysis, discussions, arguments and frustrations I finally bought a five-bedroom house, with potential to convert it into six rooms, in Berkshire. It was close to the station and had an integral garage which we wanted to convert into an en suite annex room. Although the property did not meet the three golden rules that we were taught in all property courses, I decided to go ahead with the purchase as it met my criteria for good cash flow.

Golden Rule 1 – Always buy 25% or more below market value (BMV). In other words, buy discounted properties.

This house was on the market for £350k and we bought it for £305k. There was a small discount and the deal did stack up, which was enough to make up my mind.

Golden Rule 2 – Buy a run-down property, add value and refinance after six months to pull out your funds.

This property was fully done up and the only added value was through the garage conversion.

Golden Rule 3 – Buy in the north of England for maximum yield.

This property was in the southeast as we wanted to focus on capital appreciation and were willing to pay more down south.

After mortgage and bills I made £1.5k every month, which was half way towards my target income. I decide then that I wanted to manage the property myself.

By the time I had got this property up and running I was at the end of the sabbatical. It was very frustrating as I had made progress but not met my target, so I had to eat humble pie and go back to work. I felt like a failure; I had been blasé and I was embarrassed to be at work.

Basically it was my own belief that I had failed that made me miserable. By now I had lost all interest in IT and my job and had become almost unemployable. I got assigned to a project over one and a half hours' drive from home and that gave me more motivation to achieve my goal even quicker. So after a few weeks of feeling dejected and miserable, I picked up the pieces.

Finally I stumbled on my next deal. This property was a four-bedroom terraced house which needed full works, including a new boiler, new radiators, full rewiring, new en suite, new bathroom and structural works including new lintel and kitchen. It did cost over £30k to refurbish, and we had problems when the first builder left us with a lot of incomplete work. We found another company who took over, and finally after two and a half months we got the work complete. Once the furniture packs and white goods were in the property it was good to go, and we had it fully tenanted within two weeks of completion.

Once this project was complete I was officially financially free as the property income covered my bills and living expenses. What do you think I did next? Yes, of course I resigned from my job and graduated to my full-time property investor role. It was like starting from a clean slate. I did have some experience but no funds, so I thought if I helped enough people to build up their portfolios I would meet investors along the way who would collaborate on projects and joint ventures.

From 2012 till now this has been very fulfilling and rewarding in more ways than one. Of course it has been challenging, but I've enjoyed every day of being my own boss. I don't think I have missed my job for even a moment.

Why Invest?

I invest for many reasons: cash flow, passive income, pension, retirement and capital appreciation are some words that spring to mind. And most importantly I can leverage.

Before we start getting into the technical details of property investment I would like to share with you my definition of terminology such as wealth, asset, financial freedom, ROI and passive income so you get an understanding of my perspective. Some of these definitions are taken from Kevin Whelan's *Presentation to Investors*. Kevin is a highly experienced and respected Independent Financial Advisor (IFA) based in London.

What is an asset? An asset is something that puts money in your bank account while you are asleep. You can be busy doing something else. It does not end because you are not around.

There are seven different types of asset classes:

1 **Home equity.** This is the difference between the loan (mortgage) amount and the market value of your property. Historically property prices in the UK double every seven to ten years. You can re-mortgage the house for a higher amount. The increase in the price of your property over a period of time will depend on the length of time you have been in the property, the add value you have created during this period and how well the economy is doing. These factors determine how much equity you have built in your property that you can use to raise finance again by re-mortgaging.

2 **Intellectual property.** This is knowledge you have which can be monetised by creating content via books, blogs, processes, methods, frameworks, software codes etcetera, publishing some or all of the content.

3 **Investments.** Stocks, shares, bonds, ISAs, fixed deposits, gold, silver, diamonds and any other collateral that you have invested in.

4 **Pension.** Company pensions, final salary, private pensions all provide a return on investment.

5 **Property portfolio.** A buy to let property portfolio generates rental income on a monthly basis, making property one of the most desirable asset classes.

6 **Business.** Initially you will need to invest time, but with the right systemisation it can become an asset that will generate you income without your personal time investment.

7 **Joint ventures.** Collaborate with friends and family.

Wealth for me is an abundance of good health, money, personal freedom and loving relationships.

What is passive income? It is first necessary to understand active income which you earn when you trade your time for money, for example being in a job as a permanent, temporary or contracting employee. Passive income is the opposite and it does not require your active involvement. It is income generated by assets you own that are fully managed by your own business or third party business.

Return on investment (ROI) is the cash on cash return, which in English means it is the rate of return (interest as a percentage) on the amount of money that you have invested. For example, banks are typically giving us 1–2% per annum ROI on our money, which is less than the rate of inflation so therefore your money is devaluing in the bank. It is worth less in the future than when you deposited it.

Why Invest in Property?

Property can be a vehicle to having your time freedom back. Long term property investment can give you the true financial freedom you are seeking. I have compiled ten compelling reasons to invest in property.

1   **Make your money sweat.** There is an old adage – money makes money, which is so true when you apply it to property investing in the UK. Historically in the UK, property has doubled in value every seven to ten years; this time around the cycle is a little longer, but nevertheless property will always be a good long term investment strategy. Not only does it give you a consistent cash flow every month, but the added advantage of capital appreciation is always under emphasised.

2   **Banks (ISAs/Stocks).** Yes you can invest in stocks and shares, but it is a higher risk strategy and will need a lot of specialist knowledge. ISAs typically give you around 2%–3% annual returns on your investment. If you are content with these returns then this is the right investment for you.

   Property can give you gross yields of 10% annually and a ROI of over 12% per annum, so ISAs don't come close.

3   **Plan for retirement.** As I mentioned before, the majority of over sixty-five-year-olds in the UK retire in debt.

Typically we are so busy living our life we forget to plan for our retirement. Would you be able to survive on a state pension? The maximum you can get is approximately £110 per week. Now is the time to take action and not wait till it's at your doorstep.

Also there are ways of making better use of your pension funds. You can invest in property for higher returns, but there are several dos and don'ts. You will need to speak to a pension specialist IFA.

4 **Lifestyle.** Are you living the lifestyle you always dreamed of? If you are just about making ends meet with little disposable income to enjoy with family and friends, then you need to be seriously thinking about supplementing your income through other sources. If getting another job is not an option, property investing could be the answer.

The extra income you make from property can be used to enjoy a more enriched lifestyle for you and your loved ones.

5 **Back to basics.** Human beings have three basic requirements to survive: sustenance, clothing and shelter. Because everyone needs a roof over their head, there will always be a demand for housing. The UK population is increasing at a rapid rate due to a combination of factors, not least the ever growing immigration from Europe. Due to this, property will always be in demand and property prices will rise in the long term.

6   **Demand versus supply.** Demand for property/housing in the UK is higher than supply; basic demand and supply economic principles apply. When demand outstrips supply, property prices will increase.

7   **Top ten richest people.** If you look at the top ten richest people in the world, you will see that property is the preferred asset base for the majority on the list.

8   **Wealth creation.** Property can be leveraged over a period of time. You must review your portfolio on a regular basis, refinance to buy more properties and increase your asset base, thereby creating long term wealth. Historically property has always increased in value over time and the increase contributes towards your wealth.

9   **Legacy.** In today's economic times with tough lending criteria, it is very difficult for young people to get on the property ladder. Your property investment will enable your children and grandchildren to enjoy the benefits long after you make the investment, giving them a great head start in life and the edge to progress in their careers.

10 **Freedom and choices.** The income from my rental properties has given me personal and financial freedom. The time that I have earned back from giving up my job I now utilise to run my own property business and spend with my children. I would have never imagined that this would be possible had it not been for property. I am my own boss and decide how I spend my time.

Seven Common Mistakes to avoid as a Property Investor

1   **Following the crowd.** A strategy that suits someone else may not be the ideal one for you. Think about your own situation, and more importantly what you are looking to get out of the investment, before you jump.

All investors have a fixation for buying below market value properties without actually knowing what they would yield in cash flow terms. Yes you can buy tens or even hundreds of BMV properties using this strategy, but be clear what that would achieve at the end.

2   **Not doing your own due diligence:**

- Know the market, especially when buying and flipping (adding value and selling). You need to be sure you get the timing right and that the market is not going to fall. Keep in touch with interest rate rises, inflation and economic conditions in general.

- When buying to hold you can assume that long term prices generally go up, but you must be cautious. Don't buy when the market is in a big hype, like in 2007–08, and people are paying well over the asking price due to the buying frenzy. After the crash a lot of the properties were in negative equity. This would be OK if you didn't need to refinance or sell and your rent was covering your mortgage, but a lot of people who lost their jobs were in negative equity. They couldn't afford the mortgage payments and their homes were repossessed.

- Know your area. Even if you decide to invest through a third party, you need to have done your homework. You should know the area well: demand in that area, long term growth prospects, infrastructure investment from the Government, housing plans, new employment in the area. Is the demand for housing in this area growing?

- Know your numbers. Never believe an agent's calculations on yield and returns on investment. Always do your own number crunching and add 10% contingency to your figures as a worst case scenario. If the deal still stacks up you know you cannot go wrong, but you always need to base you decisions to offer or not on the numbers. Property is a numbers game.

3 **No Plan.** Start with the end in mind. Randomly buying properties in different areas of the country is not the best strategy for having a systematic approach. Investing in property is a business and should have a business plan. At the very least it should have details on each of the following:

- Cash flow versus capital growth. Although cash flow is the most popular reason for investing, a few investors have done really well from buying new build off plan then selling when it's been built and the demand is high. Other investors have made money buying and holding in London where property can appreciate up to 20% and more in one year. It is more cash intensive, but if you do have access to more cash it would work for you.

- South versus north. Property prices in London and the southeast are a world apart from the rest of the country. However you need a different strategy for each area and knowledge of the pros and cons of the strategies to make an informed decision.

- Number of properties. I particularly don't want to own more than twenty to thirty properties making £1k–£2k net cash flow a month as the focus then changes to managing people rather than properties. My target income of £25k per month would require owning 100+ single-let properties and this is not my chosen strategy. Decide on your ideal number and plan accordingly.

- Goldmine area. I would recommend investing within one hour driving distance from home in case of emergencies for the peace of mind of knowing that you can be available if required.

- Funding. How are you going to raise funds for investing? Property owning can be an expensive business and I can guarantee that your money will run out eventually.

There are plenty of options available, including but not limited to the ones listed below:

a) Cash in the bank.
b) Refinance to release equity from your residential and other buy to let properties.

c) Unencumbered property – parents' home.

d) Inheritance – ask to receive it early so you can invest and grow this.

e) Collaborate – joint ventures with family and friends.

4 **Not being open minded.** There is a lot of media interest in the property industry. You need to be able to separate the wheat from the chaff and make your own decisions based on calculated risks rather than getting carried away by the media hype. All landlords are made out to be evil and greedy, but in my experience new generation landlords are clued up. Yes they want to make money, but they are prepared to provide quality accommodation and make repairs to the property to maintain the standard.

5 **Making assumptions.** It's easily done. You need to make your own decisions rather than taking what others say as true. Assuming that one specific strategy is better than others is a classic assumption that investors make. It comes back to doing your own due diligence.

6 **Giving up too easily.** Property is not a get rich quick scheme. It will make you rich and wealthy in the long term, but you need to give it time. I can get very impatient at the best of times, but I have realised I am not in a race. It's a journey and we need to enjoy and learn from our experience. The right mind-set and persistence will come in handy. We are very good at assuming that everyone else is doing better than us and not giving ourselves credit for our learning and small wins.

7   **Jumping on the bandwagon.** When a new strategy becomes very popular and it seems like a lot of investors are making a lot of money using this strategy, we leave what we are focused on to learn a new technique. You have lost the momentum on what you were working on and you might have been close to seeing success but now you have to start all over again. So think again before you give up what you are doing to learn a new skill or technique.

All About HMOs

Multi-let or house-share is the layman's term for HMOs (Houses of Multiple Occupation). A property is technically classified as an HMO if there are three or more tenants sharing communal areas like the kitchen and bathrooms.

Would you agree that HMOs are one of the most popular property investment strategies at the moment?

Why should I invest in HMOs? I hear you ask. Not sure if they are the best strategy for you? What is the best location? Not sure how many rooms they would need to have? How much is the minimum target for ROI and gross yield? What will the bills and other outgoings amount to? Not sure if there will be a good and steady demand from tenants in your area?

I can give you my personal top five reasons why I invested in HMOs. Generally I find that most investors relate to some or all of these:

1 **Personal Freedom.** I could not bear the fact that my time was not my own from Monday to Friday and that I had such a limited quota for holidays in a year.

2 **Quality vs Quantity.** I only needed to invest in two to three properties to get to £3,000 per month passive income. This seemed more plausible than the twenty or thirty single-let investments I would need to make up the £3,000 monthly income I needed to give up my job.

3 **Robust model.** If a single-let property is empty for a period of time, you will have to pay the mortgage from your own pocket. In HMOs you can have empty rooms but still be able to pay your mortgage. Yes your profit will be reduced, but your mortgage and bills can be covered by letting 50% of the rooms.

The HMO model also has a better chance of withstanding mortgage rate hikes, which in the current market are imminent. You can technically recycle your money with HMOs (it does take slightly longer than single-lets).

4 **Four to five times the income.** As compared to single-lets you can make four to five times the income from HMOs by renting out single rooms instead of renting a property to a single family. You will more than quadruple your cash flow and more than double your gross yield. Your ROI will be well over 12% (10% more than the banks give you).

You can make £1,000 net income per month, so technically you need three to five HMOs to become financially free (as opposed to ten to twenty single-lets).

5   **No or low voids.** Using websites like Spare room, Easy room mate and Gumtree; with good and timely management of the property you will learn to keep voids to minimum.

What are high-end HMOs and why invest in them?

A high-end HMO is a property refurbished to a high standard before it's rented out. Typically you will have fitted a new quality kitchen, added more bathrooms and en suites where possible. You will not have cut corners in the refurbishment and the rooms will all be kitted out with quality furniture and possibly flat screen TVs. The kitchen will be fitted with all appliances, bathrooms will have good tiles, shower units and sinks. There will be weekly or fortnightly cleaning and gardening services and unlimited Wi-Fi.

It is a personal question, but how would you like to live? How would you feel if you came back to a lovely clean room in a lovely clean house after a long day at work? I live in a spacious house which has been completed and decorated to a high-end specification, has good quality furniture and is homely. I have a philosophy in life: treat others like you want to be treated. I genuinely believe that if you provide quality accommodation for young professionals, you can charge a premium for it. People appreciate that nice things cost extra, and if you want the best, you will have to pay for the best. And to top it all, the returns you get are also best.

Here are ten reasons why you should consider investing in high-end HMOs for professional tenants.

1 There is a big demand for an all-inclusive package from working professionals so they know their monthly outgoings from the start.

2 Professionals appreciate good quality accommodation and are willing to pay premium rent.

3 The professional works hard and would like to go back to a nice, clean, modern house/room at the end of the day.

4 The professional mindset is that they deserve to live well.

5 As the demand outstrips supply, you will have less void periods, especially if you plan in advance and advertise the room in a timely manner.

6 Less wear and tear in the property if you have a regular cleaner going in and looking after the communal areas.

7 Professional tenants really appreciate the cleaning service and you do have tenants staying for longer.

8 The most suitable properties tend to be in residential areas which are safer and less like your typical HMO concentrated areas.

9 The tenants tend to be from decent, respectable families (like you and I).

10 They tend to be at work from Monday to Friday, 9am–5pm, which reduces heating and electricity consumption.

Property Investing

There are two very distinct aspects of investing in property: Property investment and Property development.

Property Investing

Below is a list of overarching models for property investment in operation in the UK:

1   **New build property.** These are ready-made investments and you will typically pay over the odds for them. Benefits include capital appreciation, higher rent, and fully managed solution. These are more suitable for London based properties and are a very popular strategy for overseas investors. Large UK based property developers showcase new build projects internationally, including big markets like Hong Kong, Singapore, Malaysia and Indonesia.

The apartments are sold off-plan on a price per square foot basis, sometimes even before the building work has started. The plans are all drawn up and planning permission is in place. The investor would pay in instalments and get possession of the property over a twelve to twenty-four month period. Popular projects include Battersea Power Station, Kew Bridge and Paddington. Overseas investors have traditionally seen London as a good base and demand has been constant.

As a rule of thumb you would pay a premium for a new build property and the service charges are high. The advantages are that it will be built to a good specification and will typically be near transport where private housing demand is high, so you can demand premium rent.

2 **Second hand market.** These are properties that are not new build and they account for over 90% of the market. There is more potential for getting a deal as they tend to be older, more run down properties to which you can add value before reselling.

3 **BMV or discounted properties.** These properties tend to be in the Midlands and the north of the country where general demand and prices for housing are lower than the south. The yields can be higher as you are paying less for the property.

The disadvantage is that if you live in the south you are not in a position to monitor your property and are fully reliant on the agent. Also the capital appreciation element is non-existent. However from a cash flow viewpoint it is a good strategy.

For each model there are different strategies investors can study to understand which one best suits their situation. When starting out it is always useful to focus on one or two strategies and try them out. For example, I invested my time in learning how to convert three-, four- and five-bedroom houses into professional house shares (HMOs). Other investors might want to focus on buying one- or two-bedroom flats in Guildford, just as an example, or do the rent-to-rent strategy in Liverpool. In the following chapters I will explain how you can arrive at the best investment strategy for you, but the strategies are briefly explained below:

1 **Buy to let (BTL).** This typically refers to flats and houses that are rented single family, be that to a single person or a couple with or without offspring.

2 **Houses of multiple occupation (HMOs).** In plain English, a dwelling that has three or more unrelated tenants and has shared areas like a kitchen and bathrooms is a HMO.

Although strictly speaking HMOs are a type of buy to let (BTL) investment, they are classified as specialised investments in their own right as there are different rules and regulations surrounding them.

3 **Buy to sell (BTS).** This strategy is to buy a property, add value by refurbishment and sell for a profit. It is commonly known as flipping or flips.

There are many types of flipping examples and a few are covered below.

4 **Creative strategies:**
   - Lease options
   - Assisted sales
   - Instalment contracts.

5 **Rent to rent** (also known as let to let or guaranteed rent). This works just like a corporate let where you let a property for an extended period of time and rent out the rooms to individual professionals from one or more companies.

BTL

This strategy is good for busy professionals and business owners who want a completely hands free investment. The annual return on investment is typically 3–7% depending on where in the country you invest. Returns are normally higher in the Midlands and north of the country as the property prices are cheaper.

A good example of ROI for a three-bedroom house as a BTL investment would be as follows (all prices and rent are based on averages):

Purchase price: £220k
Mortgage: (@75% LTV) £165k
Rent: £900 pm

Cash required:

Deposit: £55k
Stamp duty: £1.9k
Refurbishments: £10k (decoration, new kitchen and bathroom)
Legal fees: £2k
Total: £68.9k

Outgoings:

Monthly mortgage: (@ 3% pa) £413 pm
Letting agent fees: (@ 10% pa) £108 pm
Insurance: £30 pm
Voids: (@ 5% pa) £45 pm
Maintenance: (@ 10% pa) £90 pm
Total: £686

Cash in hand (pre-tax): £214 pm

ROI: 3.7%

HMOs

I will use the same example as above to explain ROI for HMOs.

Purchase price: £220k
Mortgage: (@ 75% LTV) £165k
Rent: £2,500 pm

Cash required:

Deposit: £55k
Stamp duty: £1.9k
Refurbishment: £40 (loft conversion, decoration, new kitchen and bathroom, one en suite)
Legal fees: £2k
Total: £100k

Outgoings:

Monthly mortgage: (@ 4.5% pa) £620 pm
Letting agent fees: (@ 10%) £250 pm
Insurance: £30 pm
Voids: (@ 5% pa) £125 pm
Maintenance: (@ 10% pa) £90 pm
Bills: £500 pm
Total: £1,615

Cash in hand (pre-tax): £885 per month

ROI: 10.6% per annum

This very simple example proves that you can treble your rental income (ROI) by turning your house into a HMO.

Flips (or buy to sell) strategy

There are different types of flipping strategies, but the essence is to buy a property, add value to it and sell it for a profit.

I have included examples of some of the popular flip strategies here:

1 Cosmetic refurbishment. This strategy is to find unmodernised houses or flats and add value by doing a refurbishment. Typically adding a new kitchen and bathroom would increase the value of the property.

2 Add one or more additional bedrooms. If you can play around with the layout, combine the lounge with an open plan kitchen and add a bedroom to the property you can make a good profit.

   To work out the cost of an additional bedroom in your goldmine area please check out the difference in price for a one- and two-bedroom flat or a three- and four-bedroom house.

3 Add an extension. Ideally a single or double storey extension will add value to the property by increasing the number of reception rooms and bedrooms.

Below is a case study of a flip project. It is also an example of a joint venture between us and another couple who we met through the property network.

A joint venture buy-refurbish-sell project.

Location: central Reading, Berkshire.

Description: A two-bedroom, two-bathroom house in a highly central location in Reading. It was run down and needed complete modernisation.

Joint venture agreement: both parties invested equal amounts of money. One hosted the mortgage and the other managed the project from start to end. The profit from the sale of the property was split 50/50.

Purchase price: £165k
Deposit: (@ 25%): £41,250
Refurbishment: £15k
Mortgage costs: £3k (6 months mortgage @ 5%)
Additional costs: £2k (legal and acquisition costs)

Total cash invested: £61,250

SP: £216k

Total Profit: £31,000 (after paying off the mortgage, total investment and deducting legal costs and agent's fees)

Investor profit: £15,500
My profit: £15,500
ROI: 25.3%

Refurbishment:

1 Painting and decoration of the house.
2 A new kitchen.
3 A new en suite bathroom had to be installed.
4 The bathroom downstairs had to be upgraded.
5 The kitchen had to be re-piped and re-plastered.
6 The garden had to be cut down and tidied up.
7 New electrics were installed in the two bedrooms upstairs.
8 New windows throughout the property.
9 New carpets throughout.

See before and after pictures below:

The old kitchen and entrance to the bathroom at the back.

The old kitchen.

The old dining room.

The old en suite.

Below are professional pictures after the refurbishment.

Property Development

Below is a list of some of the types of property development strategies that are popular in the current market.

Split title

Convert a house into two or more flats. This is also known as the freehold to leasehold strategy. You buy a house under one title and split it into two to three flats, split the titles and refinance the flats individually. See an example below.

Field Road, Reading (title split)

The property was purchased as two one-bedroom flats under one freehold title. The refurbishment will involve remodelling to create two two-bedroom flats. Legally the title deeds will be split to create two leasehold properties.

Expected gross development value (GDV) after refurbishment and remodelling works is £350k.

Financial analysis:

Purchase Price: £245k
Refurbishment/Remodel: £40k
SDLT/Legal: £7.5k
ERV: £1,700 per month
Expected GDV: £350k
Equity: £87.5k
Money Left In: £30k
ROI (post-refinance): 26% per annum

Convert commercial property into residential

A couple of years ago the Government introduced a new scheme to allow office space (B1a) to be converted to flats under the permitted development rights, which meant that planning permission would not be required. A prior approval process would need to be undertaken, which is a lot less cumbersome than planning permission and can only be refused on the grounds of highways, contamination and flooding.

There are a couple of other scenarios where you can build within permitted development rights. These are currently valid unit May 2016, but there is a general consensus in the market that this deadline will be extended.

1 Office to residential (B1a).
2 Retail unit (A1) to residential C3 (restricted up to a certain size).
3 Barn conversions to residential (personal use only).

New build

1 Buy land and apply for planning permission for house(s) and/or blocks of flats.
2 Buy a house with a big plot of land and develop two or more houses or build a block of flats.
3 Use the back garden to add house(s).

Each of these strategies can be used to make a profit. The strategy that would be ideal for you will depend on your knowledge, team of builders, time, funds, risk profile, etcetera.

If this sounds too daunting, another option is available. This option is ideal if you are a full-time professional, business owner or retired, you have equity or funds but don't have the time and/or knowledge to do it yourself. It is called armchair investing, and there are many companies in the UK that specialise in acquiring investment properties for passive/armchair investors.

There are two very big advantages of armchair investing.

1 **Time rich.** You can continue to do what you know best and leave the rest to the professionals who know how to invest your money. You will, however, need to discuss your personal requirements and make sure you are aware of all the fees and costs involved.

   Typically there are companies that do investments and development projects in collaboration with investors. Each has a unique model, and building trust and developing a working relationship is important before getting into an arrangement.

2 **Cash rich.** You can build assets and monthly cash flow by investing in property. The assets will always appreciate over a period of time and you can use the additional income to reinvest and live a better lifestyle. You will need to meet the following prerequisites to buy property.

   • Mortgage-ability. Ideally if you are PAYE or have SA302 (self-employed) accounts for three years then as long as you have a decent income you can get a mortgage.

It would be a good idea to consult an independent mortgage broker who can help you get started.

- Funds. Stating the obvious here, but you will need funds to get started. You might not have cash in the bank, but there are several other options of raising finance legally. Where there is a will there is a way.

Funding options. I am not a financial broker so will not be able to give you financial advice, but I can give you my opinion based on experience. Please get my advice backed up by a qualified financial adviser.

1 Bank savings. This is self-explanatory. It is important to note that cash in the bank gives excellent peace of mind, but will not do anything to add to your wealth.

2 Equity release. If you or your parents own your main residence you can release equity. You will need to consult a IFA/mortgage broker for financial advice.

You can discuss the pros and cons with parents and share the cash flow that you make from the investment.

3 Inheritance. If you have property and/or cash you are inheriting then ask to receive it earlier so you can invest and grow it.

4 ISAs. These typically give 2–4% ROI annually. You would be better off investing in a property which has been statistically proven to double every seven to ten years in the UK.

5   Partnering. Share the rewards with joint venture partners, who may be friends, family members or investors you have teamed up with.

6   Loan. If you have friends, siblings or parents who have the funds you can take a loan and pay them more than the banks. You can draft a loan agreement using a solicitor and pay them 5–6% returns. If you invest in the right strategy you can make over 20–25% returns, and even after the loan had been paid off you will have plenty left over.

In this chapter I will focus on showing you how to stack a HMO deal.

Deal Or No Deal

When you start looking for your first HMO investment property it is very difficult to know if a specific deal stacks up or not. Although the answer is relatively simple, most of us either over or underestimate our costs and somehow the deal doesn't stack up.

I have a simple formula to ensure that you are buying the right deal.

Return on investment (ROI). It is the single criterion that all professional investors investigate before making an offer for a property.

The way I calculate ROI can be explained in three simple steps:

1 Work out all the cash invested in the deal.
2 Work out annual net income.
3 Cash invested divided by net income then multiplied by 100 gets the % ROI.

Cash invested in the deal. This typically will include:

1 Deposit (usually 25% of the purchase price).
2 Stamp duty (1% for £250k and under and 3% for up to £500k).
3 Legal fees (£1k – £1.2k).
4 Refurbishment costs (£10k – £20k).
5 Furniture pack (approx. £2k).
6 Sourcing fees (if you use an agent).
7 White goods.

Net income. To work out the net income I use the following formula: income (rent) minus costs.

Costs typically include the following:

1 Mortgage.
2 Utilities (gas, electricity, water).
3 Council tax.
4 Broadband.
5 Sky package (optional).
6 Cleaner (optional).
7 Voids.
8 Management fees.
9 Maintenance.

In my view an annual return of 10% and above in London and the southeast is an extremely good return on your investment, considering banks will only give 1%–2%. Bear in mind this does not take into consideration capital appreciation, which in London and the southeast, as a conservative estimate, has historically been around 5%–10% per annum in the growth years.

Let me take you through an example. You are looking to purchase a property which is on the market for £295k, and you would like to make an offer of £275k. How do you know if the deal stacks up?

Is it a good deal or a great deal?

6 rooms HMO in central Reading location
Professional HMO in desirable location, near Reading station.
Self-managed

Property Details		Purchase costs	
Purchase price	275,000	Deposit	68,750
Monthly rent	3,800	Agent/lead fee	5,500
Gross yield	13.8%	Purchase costs, including legal	1,125
		Stamp duty	8,250
		Refurbishment costs	55,000
		Furniture/white goods	3,000
		Contingencies	0
		Compliance	Included
		Licence	1,000
		Cash required on purchase	**142,625**
Mortgage details		**Income**	
		Rental income	45,600
LTV	75%		
Deposit	68,750	**Expenditure**	
		Insurance	150
Total Mortgage Amount	206,250	Letting agent fee	0
Interest rate	5%	Maintenance	500
Monthly cost	859	Mortgage payments	10,313
		Void periods (@5%)	1,900
		Service charge	0
		Bills	7,200
		Net Income	**25,538**
		ROI	**17.9%**

Notes:
Bills: £600 pm (includes council tax, utilities, water, Wi-Fi, full sky package, fortnightly cleaning).
Rent: 650 x 4, 600 x 2

HMO Myths:

HMOs are very difficult to manage. The bulk of the work is when you set up the property and you have to recruit five or six new tenants. A lot of time is spent in doing the marketing and viewings, but you can organise bulk viewings. And with the help of websites like www.spareroom.co.uk you can market all the rooms in one go.

If the property is to a good standard then the tenants tend to stay, decreasing the amount of viewings over time. You can also offer a minimum six month contract.

In terms of management, there will be little maintenance work to do in the first few years on a newly refurbished.

HMO tenants don't get on with each other. Yes we have had a couple of issues with tenants in the last two to three years, but only once have we considered giving a tenant notice to leave. Therefore it is not a big issue. You need to lay down the ground rules from the start and tell the tenants that you expect professionalism at all times.

You will slowly get the hang of how to deal with tenants and issues in a professional manner. Also, the majority of the tenants will be working during the week and the only time they'll be likely to socialise will be in the evenings and weekends so there is little to argue about.

Who will stay in shared accommodation other than students or individuals on low incomes? Our tenants are young graduates, middle managers or professionals earning £25k–£30k and upwards. Shared accommodation is the norm for the current generation of twenty- to thirty-five-year-olds; they find it useful to live in shared houses because they can make friends in the local area and start their own life.

You cannot refinance HMOs. HMOs do take longer to refinance than your average single-let property, but you will make good returns from cash flow (four to five times that of a single-let property). So you are getting your money back as monthly cash flow, followed later by refinance.

You only have one exit strategy with HMOs. We do *not* box our HMOs into smaller units/rooms. Each bedroom is effectively for one tenant. Where the master bedroom is very large we will split it into two rooms, but generally we maximise rooms by adding an extension on the ground floor. So if you do need to sell your property, you will appeal to homeowners and investors alike.

HMOs are not great on cash flow after bills and other costs have been paid. You can manage the bills well by using pre-paid services like Utility Warehouse and other suppliers in the market place. You can also cap the utility payments by adding a fair usage policy in the contract. For amounts over and above that, all the tenants will have to chip in.

Too many voids. You will need to keep on top of marketing the rooms. As soon as you get notice from one tenant, you start advertising on websites such as Spareroom, Easy room mate and Gumtree. There is no room for complacency.

The Help To buy Scheme will reduce demand from HMO tenants. The HTB Scheme is catering for mainly couples who are in private rented accommodation (flats and houses). Shared accommodation tenants tend to be young single professionals and therefore there is no clash.

Statistics prove that by 2020, 30% of the UK population will be in shared accommodation.

Too much work involved. In my opinion if you have a handyman and a property maintenance company to do the small jobs and a regular cleaner and gardener going to the property they will reduce wear and tear, allowing you to be on top of issues as soon as they are raised.

Councils don't give HMO licences anymore. It depends if there is Article 4 implemented in the area. Article 4 is a directive that has been adopted by certain councils in the country where they have felt there are too many house shares which is compromising the quality of the housing in that area. Article 4 effectively takes away permitted development rights in that area and all houses in these areas that are converted to 3-6 bedroom house share will require planning permission.

Generally, if there is no Article 4 in the area, then councils are happy to work with professional landlords who are keen to keep on the right side of regulations. Recently we had an HMO officer visit one of my investor's properties to advise on HMO licence requirements. He was very complimentary on my client's approach to licensing and the specifications of the fire alarm system, fire doors, etc. The key is to work with the councils and not against them.

Creative strategies

Lease options. This strategy involves direct contact with the vendor. Typically the properties that are in negative equity qualify for this strategy perfectly. Basically any property that needs to be sold quickly and the vendor cannot wait to sell on the open market qualifies as an option.

You effectively sign an option contract with the vendor and negotiate an agreement to buy the property for a specific price on a specific date in the future. The date could be three/six/nine/twelve months, or even three/five/seven years, in the future. You will need to get all contracts drawn up by a solicitor who has experience in option contracts. This strategy will only work if it is a win-win situation for all stakeholders, i.e. for the vendor and you as the buyer. The vendor will own the property until the buyer exercises the option to buy.

The buyer has the right but not the obligation to exercise the option on the agreed date. However, to help the vendor the buyer must take over the mortgage payments immediately. The mortgage company will need to be informed and possibly change the mortgage to buy to let if you decide to rent it out or multi-let to sharers.

It is an excellent strategy for the vendor when they need to sell quickly due to personal circumstances. Typically these are as follows:

- Repossession
- Negative equity

- Moving abroad
- Probate
- Divorce
- Downsizing
- Upsizing.

Advantages for the vendor:

- They can move on with their life and don't have to pay the mortgage payments.
- They still own the property.
- Option fees can be negotiated to help the vendor. By law this can be as little as £1 with no maximum limit.
- The contracts can be customised to suit both the parties.
- The vendor can negotiate monthly payments from the buyer during the contact period (towards the purchase).

Advantages for the investor/buyer:

- No upfront money required for a deposit.
- The mortgage payments can cover themselves if you decide to rent the house.
- You can make an income by multi-letting the property to sharers.
- Property prices in the UK typically double every seven to ten years.
- You can get on the property ownership/investment ladder with a small amount of money.

You will need to go to a specialist training course if you want to do lease option contracts so you know all the legal and technical obligations.

Rent to rent is a strategy whereby you control a property with the relevant tenancy contract in place with the landlord and then multi-let the rooms to individual sharers. This is a lucrative model for persons with small investment funds seeking to replace their income through property.

You effectively take on an existing property on a corporate let contract. You are in the business of housing and relocating professional tenants.

This strategy is like offering guaranteed rent to the landlord and in return you ask for permission to sublet the rooms. You are effectively setting up a lettings agency as a specialist in corporate lettings.

The Risks:

- **You may not be able to rent the rooms.** Ensure you fully research your target area and tenants both on and off line. We had one under-performing property with a small and difficult to let room. We decided to drop the rent to well below market value to prevent voids and did not renew this contract.

- **The landlord may take the property back after your refurbishment.** This is unlikely. Most of our landlords live out of the area and are obviously only interested in receiving the monthly rent. Even if they did take it back after twelve months you would still have made an excellent return on your investment. You would, of course, remove all the items that made the property more desirable and you would no longer be managing the property, which would put the landlord right back where he started. Most landlords would be smart enough to know this.

- **Non-licensable HMO criteria may change.** Government wheels turn very slowly. Should you wish, you would have plenty of time to vacate the property before any new legislation came into practice.

- **Landlord is bankrupt.** If a repossession order is issued, the tenant (you) can apply to the courts to postpone the date for two months and then issue your tenants with notice to quit. The court may recommend a further postponement, if possible, to the mortgage company.

The landlord could well become a distressed seller, which could be an opportunity for you to purchase the property cheaply, although the mortgage company would be obliged to try and sell for the maximum value. There is a slight risk that if the tenants did have to move out within their contracted term they could, in theory, sue you for losses they sustain through moving, but we consider this to be a very small risk. You can find more information at the Protection of Tenants Act 2010.

- **Landlord dies.** Should the landlord die, initially this would make no difference to your tenancy agreement. The responsibilities of the landlord will be transferred to the new owner of the property. In the first instance this will be the executor, and then it will be whomever the property is sold or transferred to. In theory you should be able to continue paying rent as you were previously, but in practice bank accounts belonging to the deceased may be frozen. If this is the case you should keep the money safe in an escrow bank account and forward it to the new landlord as soon as you get the details. Family members of the deceased landlord may try and convince you to pay rent to them, but it could be that they are not legally entitled to it.

The new owners may wish to sell the property fast, which again could be a great opportunity for you.

I will not be covering the nuts and bolts of the strategy in this book. All I can say is that you will need training and it's a great strategy if you have a small amount of funds and more time.

Assisted sales. You create a win-win situation by working directly with the seller. For example, the vendor needs to achieve a specific price on the sale of the property and the property is not selling because it needs modernisation. You agree to help them if they agree to share a percentage of the profit from the sale with you. Without the refurbishment the property will not sell, so the vendor has no other choice,

All the T&Cs are agreed and signed in a deed of trust. You can also apply a restriction on the title deeds of the property using an RX1 form. A solicitor will charge you a nominal fee to process the restriction.

You spend the money doing the refurbishment. Once the property is sold you get your share as agreed.

Ten top tips for property investing in the UK

1   **Cash flow is King.** Always invest for cash flow, and if you can invest in an area where you can benefit from capital growth, it's a bonus. The focus should always be cash flow.

2   **Do your due diligence on the area.** Always invest within a one hour driving distance from your primary residence. I once made the classic mistake of investing in Coventry which is just over 100 miles from me. Initially I was making good profit, but eventually tenant problems persisted and the management company disbanded. For the next year we received little or no rent and the tenants trashed the place soon after we had refurbished it. Don't rush into investing in an area that you know little about.

3   **Focus on one, or a maximum of two, strategies.** I knew that HMOs were ideal for me as I wanted to replace my income from my job within a year. Know your goal and have a plan to achieve it.

Also ensure that the strategy you have picked plays to your strengths. Personally I am a people person, am good at high level business strategy and have a 'Star' profile in wealth dynamics. Therefore I enjoy public speaking and promoting my business, but I'm not great at detail. I wasted time researching the rent to rent strategy when it clearly was not playing to my strengths, and eventually I realised it wasn't the right strategy for me and my profile.

4   **Estate agents.** Use estate agents to find you your ideal deal. They make a living by selling properties and you can leverage that knowledge to your benefit. Get to know them, tell them your criteria and they will find you the right property – eventually.

5   **Power team.** Every property investor will need a builder, handyman, solicitor, mortgage broker, book keeper, accountant – the list goes on.

We've had builders who went bankrupt during one of our refurbishments. Another of our builders moved to South Africa. If you're not happy with your existing team, keep looking. After all these years I have now found the best mortgage broker money can buy. He has managed to refinance three of my HMO properties in a very short space of time and for a reasonable fee.

6   **Networking.** Tell everyone from the postman to your pharmacist, your cleaner to your neighbour, what you do. You never know where your next deal will come from.

7   **Run it as a business.** Even if you have a full-time job and you do property investing part-time, work towards systemising your buying, renting and maintenance. This will eventually free you up to buy more properties.

8   **Review your portfolio every three to six months** to ensure it meets your property and personal goals. For example, I am in the middle of an eight-bedroom HMO deal as I wanted to double my cash flow. My first couple of HMOs have given me personal freedom and the ability to live

life on my terms; this HMO will give me the ability to plan for my children and provide them with better opportunities.

9   **Trust your instinct.** Don't base your investing decisions on what other people are saying. For example, a lot of investors I meet ask me how I manage my HMOs as it seems too much hard work. You won't know unless you Also if you want to sweat your asset for more, then you will need to put in the hours initially. There is no such thing as a free lunch.

10 **Take Action.** It's the only way you will learn. Don't be afraid to make mistakes. Money will not buy you real 'on the job' experience. As long as you have done the due diligence you will need to take calculated risks. There is no guarantee in property, or any other business for that matter, so trust yourself and the time you have invested, the knowledge you have gained, and take the plunge.

THE RICH FORMULA TO FINANCIAL FREEDOM

How will complete novices learn to invest their time and money so they can be cash rich and time rich for the rest of their lives?

I have created for you a personalised RICH Formula – Rich in money, mindset and lifestyle. To help you implement your RICH Formula I have broken down the elements into four chunks.

R – Research
I – Invest
C – Create (a plan) and Collaborate
H – How and Housekeeping

I believe you can achieve financial independence in three to five years by following this step by step approach. You need to have a deadline in mind to keep the momentum going.

Research

You should spend the first six months of your property investing journey doing research. Essentially you need to work out your starting point and your end point and fill in the gaps. At the end of this phase you will be convinced that your money is better off being invested in property than in the bank. You will then be ready to move to the next phase of plan and prep. Once you have done the preparatory work it will quickly gather momentum, now you have set the ball rolling.

There is a three step approach all investors need to go through before they start to build (or expand) their property portfolio:

1 Fact finding
2 Research
3 Produce an outline plan.

Fact finding. This stage involves knowledge gathering, research and all the background work you need to do before starting the investing process.

The first step is to go through your income and expenses, assets and liabilities. These can be logged on a simple spreadsheet with tabs for each and will help you to understand your existing financial position before venturing into a new business.

At this stage it would help to consult a wealth manager and a mortgage broker. They don't normally charge for consultations and are good starting points for finding out how you can use your existing asset base to get started.

By the end of this exercise you will know how much additional passive money you need every month either to replace your income or support your lifestyle choices.

Research. Finding and financing your deals are the two skills you will need to master as a property investor. The nine step plan below will help you hone your deal finding skills.

To start your own research into local property prices you need to spend at least an hour a day following these steps:

1 Free up your evenings to do research and due diligence in your surrounding areas.
2 Go to the Rightmove website (www.rightmove.co.uk) and start looking at property prices in your area.
3 Compare these with the prices in your neighbouring town.
4 Start to look at rentals in your and your neighbouring towns.
5 Compare to see which town can achieve better yields. Yield is a very simple calculation: annual rent divided by purchase price of the property.
6 Compare sold prices in the different towns.
7 Look at a 10–20 mile radius from your house and compare prices, rents and yields.
8 Arrange viewings on the weekends with estate agents and tell them you are an investor.
9 Do this for a four–six week period to get a feel for the market.

While the research phase is in progress document all the key findings made at this stage. This will reveal the plan that will then be put into action. Some of the activities, like viewing properties and deal analysis, should be done in parallel with the research to allow you to get a feel for the different micro niche areas in local towns. Start to track specific properties and check how long they take to sell and rent. By now you should have an idea of property prices, rentals and yields within a 10 mile radius.

Additional actions required:

1 Ascertain demand for tenants. Websites like www.rightmove.co.uk, www.spareroom.co.uk and www.easyroommate.com allow you to gauge rental demand in an area. The latter two websites allow you to get in touch directly with the tenants. These websites specialise in rooms rather than houses and apartments.

2 You can ascertain the tenants/properties ratio by looking at the rooms available versus rooms wanted. This will help you work out if the area has good demand for rooms.

3 Check out competition. To work out your own Unique Selling Point (USP) you will need to know room prices, room sizes, quality of the houses, location. Work out how quickly the rooms rent by tracking specific rooms so you can create your own brand and stand out from the crowd.

4 Produce dummy adverts. When working out if a specific area/street is popular with sharers you can place dummy adverts on www.spareroom.co.uk and www.easyroommate.com to judge the response.

5 Once you are confident then you can go ahead with the sale if your offer gets accepted. You must also be aware that you will need to move quickly if the deal is good.

6 Get a dummy email address. You can create a dummy email address for property related queries so they are separate from your personal and work emails.

7   Pose as a dummy tenant to check out the quality of rental properties on the market. You will be able to book appointments with landlords/agents on www.spareroom.co.uk and www.easyroommate.com. This will help you work out your USP over your competition and you can demand higher rents as a result.

8   Discover the average time it takes to rent and/or sell a property. If your strategy is to buy, add value and sell you will need to know average selling time in the area and factor this into your calculations.

I have listed three tried-and-tested tips for finding good deals:

1   Install Firefox browser which is compatible with an application called Property Bee. This allows you to find out how long a certain property has been on the market for sale and/or rent. Any properties that have been on the market for three to six months are good candidates for a price reduction as the vendor may be keen to sell.

2   When talking to the agents ask if there are properties that are sold subject to contract (STC) but the sale is likely to fall through. The vendor in such cases is more than likely to be in a chain and would welcome buyers who can move quickly and rescue the situation.

3   Un-mortgage-able properties, which will be very run down properties with no usable kitchen and/or bathroom, flats with leases of less than thirty years,

houses with subsidence, dilapidated properties, can only be bought for cash. You can achieve discounts on cash purchases, which can then be fixed and mortgaged.

To help deepen your knowledge further you will need to do more research in the same areas.

Outline your plan. Based on what money you need and a realistic timescale, you can outline a plan of what your property business will look like.

Identify one to two suitable strategies. Based on the research of property buying and selling processes, rental yields, etcetera, identify at least a couple of strategies that would suit you.

How much investment is required for your first deal? How can you raise funds? Identify investors and joint venture partners.

Private investors are those who provide you with funds on a fixed return basis for a fixed period, typically ranging from 6% plus per annum. Joint venture partners are those who invest all or most of the funds into the deal while you do all the work, from acquisition to project management and renting/selling the property. Then you split the profit.

Output:

1 Deal analysis report and spreadsheet.
   Please create a report that includes your ideal deal in your area. Include location, a realistic purchase price, refurbishment costs, yield and ROI. Also produce a deal

analysis spreadsheet that you can use as a due diligence test base for all deals before you put offers in. We have a generic version we use that helps us with deals in all areas.

2   Area analysis report.
    This report will compare the rents and property prices in the two areas you have researched. Also include advantages and disadvantage of investing in each of these areas.

3   Tenant analysis profile.
    Please include your ideal tenant profile.

Invest

By now you will have some confidence in your deal finding skills, so it is time to gain additional skills while continuing to sharpen your abilities. You will need to invest in your education. In addition to the technical knowledge you will need to hone your mindset and motivation and identify your areas of strength and weakness. The second half of year one will be spent adopting and eventually mastering some of the disciples below.

Below is my five step proven formula for investing in yourself:

1   **Education.** There are many courses that offer intensive training in property investing techniques and strategies. I would recommend the ones that run across a six to twelve month period and offer a supportive environment

and/or ongoing coaching during that period. I've done a few weekend courses which were very informative and intensive, but I was back at my desk on the Monday morning, overwhelmed and pretty much left to my own devices.

Please be aware that a few courses, without naming and shaming any specific property educational company, tend to over exaggerate the discounts they are achieving in property prices. They boast about getting 40%–50% discounts on deals, but please do not get hung up about getting X% discount. If the deal stacks up at market price, put your offer in. Some of the course content also makes property investment look and sound like it is very easy to do. It can be simple to understand in theory, but more difficult to put into practice.

These days you can get a lot of the information you need at the click of a button.

2 **Networking.** This is an excellent way to keep in touch with property market developments and meet like-minded investors. There are many property related events throughout the country offering excellent value for money as tickets range from £10–£20 for an evening. There will typically be one or two speakers and a mortgage broker update, with plenty of networking opportunities in between. This is a great way to have an ongoing education at a fraction of the cost and I would thoroughly recommend you attend once a week if you are keen to progress your property investing career.

This is also an excellent way to build your own power team. This includes builders, broker, solicitor, handyman, lettings agent, wealth manager and scouring agents.

Your evenings should be spent reading articles in property magazines. I subscribe to *Your Property Network* (*YPN*) and *Property Investor News* (*PIN*). They include up-to-date information on changes in legislation and real case studies of normal people, their journeys and deals.

3 **Mentoring.** This is a fast track option for those looking for an early exit from their current situation. You are effectively paying for your mentor's experience and will avoid all the classic mistakes. Mentors will help you reach your goals by creating a plan with you, working out the gaps in skills and training you towards implementing your plan. At the very least they will help you in these areas:

- Accountability. This is the single most important reason why you should invest in a mentor. Property can be a lonely journey and you need ways to keep on track.

  Your mentor will hold you responsible for your actions within a realistic timescale and ensure that you have the moral support you need.

- Motivation. There are times when it gets hard and it is important to get motivational support to carry on with the task on hand. There will be times when you don't get the deal you really wanted; the mortgage offer has not come through as expected; your funding pipeline is dry and you need funds; and you will wish you had the right guidance from an experienced investor who has had to deal with similar situations before.

- Momentum. Life often gets in the way and keeping the momentum is important, especially if you are under time pressure.

  Start with the end goal in mind. Having the plan in front of you is effectively like putting your destination in a satellite navigation system: you will have different choices in front of you and you can make decisions with guidance from your mentor.

- Draw up a dream chart. Some of you will really enjoy this and others will find it difficult. Some of us have never given it a thought or think it's being too greedy. Either way it will stretch your imagination.

- Educate. Having the right technical knowledge is very important and your mentor will train you on the job. The property market is always changing and specific strategies are more relevant in one economy than another. They will also provide you with the right support environment, which is the key to success.

4 **Mastermind group.** Invest time in creating or joining a locally based group of seasoned property investors. Working closely with this group will help you feel part of something; you will be able to learn from their mistakes,

create long term working relationships and collaborate on projects. I have created a mastermind group in my goldmine area and we analyse deals together and help each other move forward in our investing journeys. It is a very supportive environment.

5 **Massive action.** You will need to immerse yourself completely in the subject and it will temporarily consume your life. However it will all be worth it.

You need to keep the momentum going. Have daily goals and weekly targets. Create and monitor KPIs like number of viewings and offers made, investor meetings, funds raised.

Below are my five top disciplines required to be a full-time property investor. If you are planning on getting into property investing as a full-time career I would recommend additional mindset tips for success.

1 **Belief.** It is very important to invest in your mindset. It is proven that the brain responds to repetition. You need to feed your brain with positive thoughts, which will lead to words and then to action (in the right direction).

The two different mindsets are the victor and victim. It is very important to have an 'above the line' mindset to become successful. Above the line you have control of the situation, and below the line is when you blame others for the situation.

O – Ownership
A – Accountability
R – Responsibility

B – Blame

E – Excuses

D – Denial

2   **Books.** When I quit my job and started to work on my property business it was very lonely. From managing a team of twenty plus to working alone in my home office was not an easy transition for me as I am very much a people person.

I had to develop the right mindset to keep my energy levels high on days when it was proving to be hard work. I had to do some soul searching at times when nothing was going my way. Books not only give you the technical knowledge you need, but they also show you real life examples of people who have successfully given up their day job and work full-time in property.

Continuous education is a must to help you in your journey. Below is a useful list of books that have helped me in my journey:

Rich Dad, Poor Dad by Robert Kiyosaki. This is the one book I can truly say has given me a new perspective of my working life. I didn't know, or I guess it didn't register, that there were ways of making a living other than a 9–5 job. This book made me realise that you can create income by generating assets which eventually replace your job income and become financially independent.

This was what I had been wanting to do for a couple of

years and didn't really know where to start. This book gave me insights and ideas of how to reinvest my money instead of letting it devalue in the bank.

Although we had invested in property previously I didn't realise that I could make a living out of this full-time. I can honestly say that this book changed my life for the better and gave me the opportunity to live life on my own terms.

Eat That Frog by Brian Tracy. The best tip I can give you from this book is to do the job you hate the most (but is probably very beneficial to your business) first thing every day. I have taken this advice and do my filing and invoicing every Monday.

Who Moved My Cheese? By Spencer Johnson. This book brings to light the fact that we live in a fast changing world, and to survive and be successful our business needs to be able to adapt very quickly. The property market is very much like that and we need to be on top of the property news and trends. Be proactive rather than reactive.

The Compound Effect by Darren Hardy. This book changed my life by helping me become more disciplined than I have ever been. I now have a morning routine that keeps me happy and positive for the rest of the day, even in the face of adversity. At a difficult time of my (personal) life this book helped me focus and appreciate all the things I am and should be grateful for, always.

The Seven Habits Of Highly Effective People by Stephen Covey. In the book the author suggests that if we want to be successful we should incorporate seven habits that will help us achieve our goals quicker.

Think And Grow Rich by Napoleon Hill. This is an inspirational book and gives the reader numerous insights into how to develop the mindset of a rich person: rich in money, wealth and life.

Entrepreneur Revolution by Daniel Priestley. This is an excellent insight into the habits and thinking of the new age entrepreneur. It reveals interesting facts about how our monkey brain thinks and how to overcome that and develop an empire-building mindset.

Property Experts' Money Making Secrets by Manni Chopra. Yes, I published this book in 2012 in the early stages of my full-time property investing journey. It is a useful read for beginners and experienced investors alike. It gives you an insight into how you can use property to make £1,000 per month additional income while doing a day job.

It is essentially a series of interviews with successful property entrepreneurs in the UK who reveal different strategies they have used to climb the property ladder.

3 **Self-discipline.** In the book *Psychology Of Achievement*, Brian Tracy explains why self-discipline is the most important ingredient to success.

This is the one habit, if mastered well, which will be your

path to success. All highly successful entrepreneurs, like Brian Tracy, Darren Hardy, Napoleon Hill, have named this on the top of their list of must have attributes.

During my journey I found the following self-disciplines to be most useful. My morning routine consists of daily goal setting, attitude of gratitude, abundance mentality and yoga. Each day of the working week has been given a focus. Mondays I focus on my personal portfolio: filing, logging all expenses, systemising and banking. Tuesday and Thursday mornings are for investor calls, and in the afternoons I focus on the business, team meetings, documenting processes. Wednesday I have dedicated to marketing, blogs, social media updates, video blogs, etc. Fridays have an investor focus with meetings, updating databases, telephone and Skype calls.

Over a period of time I have learnt that having a default diary is the only way to maximise your productivity and focus more time on systemising the business. A typical day in my working week is as follows:

MONDAY

6:10 wake up.

6.30–7 daily goals, affirmations and meditation. I write my top five personal and work goals daily and my top three most valuable priorities (MVP). MVPs are the tasks I need to get done even if nothing else gets done.

7–7.30 yoga.

7.30–8.05 drop kids at school.

8.05–8.15 attitude of gratitude. In this session I remind myself of all the things I am grateful for, including my loving family, relationships, friendships, money, lifestyle and health.

8.15–9.15 walk.

9.15–10 shower and breakfast.

10–11 filing, invoices and banking, log business expenses for last week. These tasks I normally hate doing so I get them done first thing in the week then they are out of the way.

11–11.30 emails.

11.30–1 document one personal portfolio process.

1–1.30 lunch.

1.30–2.30 review and allocate resources to maintenance of all properties.

2.30–3.30 manage adverts and fill rooms.

3.30–4 identify investors to contact in the week, add to customer databases (follow ups), emails.

4–6 kids pick up, quality time with family.

6–9 listening to radio, emailing and family time/networking event.

9–10 read book/article/property magazine.

4 **Affirmations (I am...).**To help you start believing in your dreams you will need to programme your brain by repetitive messages.

I have used affirmations in my journey to help me believe that my dreams, however big, can and will come true. A couple of examples below will help you write your own affirmations:

The About Face India anti-aging clinics in Mumbai are making Rupees. 1 Lakh (Indian currency equivalent to £1k) in daily sales from January 2015.

I successfully published my book *Cash Rich, Time Rich* in summer 2015 and it has become an Amazon best seller.

Output

1 Daily routine/default diary.
2 Dream chart.
3 Power team.

Create (a Plan) and Collaborate

This will take you into the first half of year two. By the end of this phase you will have a plan based on the knowledge and learnings from the Research phase, your beliefs and mindset.

Where would you want to be in three years' time? This is the time to be bold, think big and write down your end game plan.

Investing in property is a business and should have a business plan. At the very least it should have details on each of the following topics:

1 **Funding options.** How are you going to raise funds for investing? There are plenty of options available. Please choose two or three suitable channels from the following for funding your deals:

- Cash in the bank.
- Home equity. Using home equity is the easiest way to raise money if you have a low loan to value ratio on your house. You will need to revalue your home through an agent and by looking at comparable houses in the area.
- Refinance to release equity from any other buy to let properties you own.
- Unencumbered property – take a mortgage on your parents' home and take on responsibility for the mortgage payments.
- Inheritance – ask to receive it early so you can invest and grow this.
- Collaborate by doing joint ventures with family and friends. Always use a solicitor to produce a legal joint venture agreement and include all conditions as agreed by both parties. Your joint venture partner can put in 70–100% of the funds and you can negotiate to split the profit 50/50%, 60/40%, 70/30% or whatever suits both your needs. Under new a new directive by the UK Financial Conduct Authority (FCA) ruling PS13/3 you cannot publicly promote joint venture opportunities to an audience

unless they are certified as High Net Worth Individuals (HNWIs) or Sophisticated Investors.

- Crowd property funding. Please check out crowdproperty.co.uk for prerequisites and how the process works.
- Bridging – this is an alternative to getting a mortgage. A lot of auction properties are bought using this method of funding. Most bridging companies provide 70–90% funding on your projects if you meet their deal stacking criteria. They typically charge you anything from 1–2% per month interest on the loan and there are additional entry and exit fees. Bridging mainly works for investors who want to add value to properties and sell them for a good profit. There are a couple of companies I have used, and if you get in touch with me I can guide you based on your requirement.
- Private investor. Typically funds in the bank are being devalued as the interest does not keep abreast of the rate of inflation. Investors are typically looking for a better return on their investments. If you know friends and family who have savings in the bank you can discuss this option with them and draw up a professional loan agreement backed by first or second charge on the property.
- Pension funds. Do you have an under-performing pension that you can sell to raise finance? There are legal ways of using pension funds to invest in specific types of property, and you can use your own and other people's pensions. This industry is a mine field and I am not a qualified IFA, so I recommend you consult

your wealth manager to discuss feasible options. Alternatively get in touch with me and I will direct you to the right person.

- Stocks and shares.
- Parents' bank. Your parents may have a property and it is possible that they are close to paying off the mortgage or it is unencumbered. You can discuss going into a collaborative agreement with them. You put in the time, they supply the funds, and you jointly own your first BTL/HMO property.
- Personal loans. Depending on your credit rating you can withdraw money very quickly. However you need to work out your monthly payments compared to the rent you will receive and see if you can get a positive cash flow after deductions.
- Credit cards. This strategy is not for everyone due to high interest charges, but they can be useful for refurbishment costs or raising the initial deposit. You can find a list of the best credit cards on www.moneysupermarket.com which searches for cards that offer cash into your account or 0% on purchases, but they can affect your credit rating so please watch out for how much credit you have.

If you don't have access to any of these you can collaborate with friends and family members who might have access.

2 **Investment strategy.** Follow One Course Until Success (FOCUS).

There are many strategies available and we are always searching for the shiny new penny. It is important to understand which strategy best suits your requirements and stick to one, or a maximum of two, to ensure success. Being a 'Jack of all trades and master of none' will not get you anywhere and will overwhelm you.

When I took a sabbatical from work in 2010 I had one goal in mind: to replace my income before the end of one year so I didn't have to go back to work. I knew at that point the HMO strategy would be most suitable, and I was passionate about giving professionals a good standard of accommodation. I enjoy living well myself so I knew that high-end HMOs would suit my personality and give me a good income in a short space of time.

Similarly you need to know your financial freedom amount and the timescale you want to achieve it in. This will dictate the best strategy for you.

The only negative side of educational courses is they can overwhelm and confuse you. When you hear stories of people becoming very successful in a different strategy to your strategy of choice your mind starts to play games with you. You wonder if you should reconsider your position or diversify into a different strategy. Keep your focus on the right one for you and have faith in yourself.

3   **Goldmine area.** There are several factors that influence the right investment area for you. These include the amount of funds you have access to, your lifestyle, how much time you can commit, whether you are comfortable investing far away and whether you have family/children commitments.

There are no right or wrong answers, just choose what suits your situation. I invest within 30–40 minutes driving distance from home. I am looking for capital growth in addition to cash flow and I want to be able to get to all my properties in case of an emergency.

I would recommend sticking to one, maybe two, areas so that you can maximise your knowledge. Randomly buying properties in different areas of the country is not the best way to have a systematic approach. Learn from my mistakes. When we first bought properties we had no strategy, so we've ended up with flats in different parts of London. If we were to do it again we would be selective.

4   **Number of properties.** I would want to own twenty to thirty properties making £1k–£2k net cash flow a month. My target income of £25k per month would require owning 100+ single-let properties and this is not my chosen strategy. It's not about the number of properties you own, but the quality of the investment. The cash flow and ROI are the key indicators. Decide on your ideal number of properties and plan accordingly.

One decision you need to make is whether you have the time to find the right investment properties actively or would like to work with a company to help you. There are specialist companies in the UK for armchair/passive investors and you will need to do your due diligence to find the right one for you.

Working out your goldmine area is key to finding the right company to work with. There are typically companies that specialise in the north of the country, the south and the Midlands.

5 **Quality versus quantity.** There is a mindset that the more properties you own, the richer you are. You cannot compare the wealth of two investors, one of whom owns ten properties in London and the other ten in the Midlands or north of the country.

In my view it is all about the cash flow you can make from each property, with capital appreciation the icing on the cake.

6 **Time.** There are several ways in which you can invest in property. Some of the most successful business partnerships have been those where one partner is working full-time or running an established business and the other is expanding and managing their property portfolio. It works well as you have a steady flow of income to reinvest into property and access to mortgages.

If you are single then find a business partner whom you can work with to grow your portfolio. Decide who will work and who will take up property full-time. As mentioned, you also have the option to work with an armchair investment company who can help you create a property portfolio. Time and funds are the two most important criteria that will shape your property business.

7 **Direct marketing versus estate agents** (or both). A lot of the property educational courses teach us how to focus on doing door-to-door leafleting or advertising in the newsagents and local newspapers to make direct contact with vendors. The idea is to cut the agents out of the picture and negotiate directly, but it is important to propose an ethical win-win solution to the vendor's problem. A lot of creative solutions can only be offered directly to the vendor as agents are not trained in this specialist knowledge.

8 **Criteria.** Define your deal criteria. My minimum criteria was three bedrooms and two reception rooms for under £250k and four bedrooms with two reception rooms for £300k. You need to know what you are looking for.

The bottom line is to take action. Continue to view properties and make offers (not necessarily 25% BMV).

9 **Collaborate.** To get to where you want to be, you will need to work with others. Partner up with an investor with complementary skills. To find your ideal working partner you will need to work out your areas of strengths and weaknesses, and then find a business partner with complementary skills. Another aspect is to find a partner on a time-funds basis; you may have the time and they have the funds, which is the ideal working relationship.

Taking a talent dynamics profile test will help you find out whether you have more of a high-level creator brain or a good eye for detail, or a bit of both. I did the Roger Hamilton Profile Test, but there are many tests on the market.

Output

1 Business Plan.
2 Potential JV partners list.
3 Talent dynamics profile report.

Housekeeping

My proposal is that the HMO route is the quickest route to financial wealth and freedom. At this stage you have your own strategy so you will need to break it down in a similar manner. In terms of timing you are now in year two.

To invest in HMOs there are a few prerequisites. You will need funds for a deposit, restructure and refurbishment, stamp duty and legal fees. If you don't have the cash upfront there are several ways of raising the funds (Section 4.3). Typically you will need £100k for two property purchases in the Midlands and north. To buy two properties in the southeast you will need at least £200k.

You will need to ensure that you are mortgage-able, or collaborate with a friend/family member who is. Try and secure a mortgage with no early redemption penalty (ERP) so you can refinance after refurbishment is complete.

Property one. Search for properties with a minimum of three bedrooms and two reception rooms. Ideally the kitchen should be big enough for a breakfast bar/dining table. Typically the house will need modernising so you can add value. You should look at creating an additional room to make a higher return on your investment. The idea is to get an HMO mortgage, refurbish then refinance to get some of your money out, which will be needed to finance your next purchase.

Typically the property should make you between £800 and £1,000 per month net income (after mortgage and costs, pre-tax).

Typical floor plan:

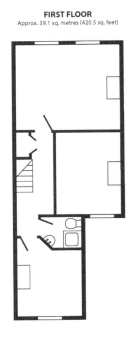

Property two (year three). Once property one has been operational for six months you can apply to refinance. You should be able to pull out the funds you used to refurbish and recycle the cash for the next purchase, but you will need to leave some funds tied in. To fund your second purchase you could reuse the funds you have released from property one for the deposit, but will potentially need access to additional funds if the property needs a large refurbishment.

Follow the same pattern and you will be able to get another lot of £800–£1,000 per month net cash flow. So by the end of year two you have a total cash flow of £1,600–£2,000 per month.

Property three (end of year three/start of year four). You will need to refinance property two and recycle the funds for refurbishment.

By the time the third property is up and running you will have £2,500 and £3,000 net cash flow per month, and this is when you have achieved true financial independence.

This example makes a few assumptions:

1   Property one and two have increased in value as a result of the added value process.
2   At refinance, property one and two have been valued at the price you expected.
3   You have been able to secure mortgages for all properties with no early redemption penalties.
4   You have access to funds.
5   You have access to deals.

Worst case scenario. You have not been able to value the property/properties at the price that will enable you to pull out the funds to secure properties two and/or three. In that case it will take longer than six months to refinance and it will be more like a five year cycle to achieve financial independence.

Housekeeping. To have freedom from your portfolio you will need to invest time to systemise and document your business processes. This includes marketing the properties, tenant finding and referencing, checking in and out, monthly inspections, inventory, logging and managing maintenance jobs. This is to free you up, eventually giving you the flexibility to live life on your own terms and pursue your passions.

Following the RICH formula you are now financially abundant. It is time to focus on your personal self, your personal vision and ask yourself some soul searching questions. What does true happiness mean for you? My personal vision is to help individuals and families experience true wealth through financial abundance. Have you ever asked yourself this question? How will you be truly happy?

Most of us are so entangled in the time-for-money trap that we don't ask ourselves this very important question. We grow up thinking this is how we are supposed to live our lives. We are so entrenched in our day-to-day lives that we don't see an opportunity even when it's staring in our face, as illustrated by the story I am about to share with you.

Believe it or not I had the opportunity to leave my job in 2003 when my second child was born and I did hand in my resignation. But then I asked to withdraw it. What was I thinking? Why do you think I did that? Do you think I asked myself what would make me truly happy?

Romey was running a recruitment consultancy back then and doing well so I could have afforded to leave my job and be with the kids full-time. However subconsciously I was afraid that if Romey's business packed up we would all be in a soup. My insecurities about money started to surface; I believe this was all to do with my limiting beliefs around financial security from childhood.

So I went back to a two hour commute to central London every day. Why, when most of my salary went to pay for my travel and childcare? It was just the security of knowing I had a job and we wouldn't starve, because my mindset was not open at the time and also I didn't know how to replace my salary.

Using my story, I show that we all need to expand our minds so we can understand how to change our perspective and believe that we can make a change.

My eleven-year-old was discussing career options for her and told me off as she thought my ambition was for her to get a profession focused on money. Little does she know about life with no money. She has always lived a privileged life and doesn't know what it's like to struggle. Don't feel guilty about wanting to make more money. It's what you do with the money that will make a difference in your life.

This is the time to get your dream chart out and start ticking off some of your dreams as you accomplish them.

I will give you an example of what true wealth is to me:

1   Time freedom to be my own boss. My dream isn't sitting on a beach all day sipping champagne as I would get bored too quickly – I suffer from 'ants in my pants syndrome'. I can do it for a couple of days, but it would drive me up the wall eventually.

2   I am thankful I get the time to walk my dog every day in the fresh air of Burnham Beeches which is a nature reserve a few hundred yards from my home. I feel fulfilled as I can drop the kids off and pick them up from school, watch their rugby and netball matches and be there for them. Also I have time to meditate, spiritually discover myself, pursue business opportunities and catch up occasionally with friends and family.

3   Money freedom to have a passive income that exceeds my expenses, can support my lifestyle and let me have fun. To be able to take short city breaks in the school holidays and family holidays exploring the world in luxury and style.

4   Family time to be there for my husband, kids and extended family, supporting and encouraging them through difficult times in their lives.

5   Help to motivate, mentor and coach others to the route of financial and time freedom.

6   Spiritual time to invest in discovering how to better myself as a person, grow spiritually, meditate to become a better person: a more loving, peaceful, kind, patient and accepting human being.

7   Investing in my home. Having just converted my garage into a home office, my next home project is to landscape the garden and then fit a new kitchen next year. I love decorating and making my home look and feel more beautiful.

8   Invest in my potential to grow my skills as a speaker so I can help many more people experience true wealth through financial abundance.

9   Have more fun. Deep down I had a dream of being a Bollywood star. I would like to attend drama and dance lessons just for fun and feel like a star from within, or go on a girlie holiday with a couple of my close girlfriends.

Exercise 2: Please grab a pen and paper now and write down what truly makes you happy. How could you become happier in your life with more money? Ask yourself, if money was no object what would you want to do?

Output – Fun and enjoyment.

Success Stories

Below I have shared with you success stories of normal people who have become financially free due to property investing. A couple of these are our clients with whom I have personally shared the journey.

James Schumann. James has been a full property investor since the summer of 2014. He has bought a number of HMOs in London which are fully managed by a letting agency using a single assured tenancy contract (AST). This means there is a main tenant who is the signatory on the contract and is responsible for managing the flow of other tenants. The lettings agency does rent collection and maintenance.

James did not have ready cash to fund these purchases and his story goes as follows. He bought a derelict house in a fantastic community called Bonnington Square in Vauxhall (South London) in 1998 purely for himself and friends to live in, not as an investment. The property's background was that all the inhabitants of the square had been evicted in the 1980s as it was to be demolished in order to make playing fields for a nearby school (inconceivable today), but the process was stopped by Thatcher and so the houses sat empty. They all became squats, and after twelve years' ownership the squatters formed housing co-ops and gained the right to live in the properties.

The square had (and still has) a wonderful community, with its own bakery and café. The housing co-op sold some of the houses off at auction to raise money to renovate other houses, and James bought his house that way. He lived there until 2003, and when he left London he decided to keep the house and rent it out.

In 2012 James got involved in an arts project for which he needed significant funding. This gave him the motivation to look at how to increase his income, which led him ultimately to Simon Zutshi's Mastermind Programme. During that programme James released equity from his Vauxhall house (which had substantially increased in value) to purchase and renovate properties in London, Oxford and Bracknell to run as shared houses (HMOs).

James wanted the freedom not to have to sit in an office all day; to be able to travel and run worthwhile environmental and arts projects. James spent the entire British winter of 2014/2015 in the Canary Islands, running his property business from his iPhone.

James's advice to those looking to start in property is to immerse yourself in the area you want to know about – talk to people who have already done it and been successful. Read books, watch videos, join forums, do courses – be a sponge. Start taking action, then keep taking action, even when you have doubts and fears. It helped James to have a coach to keep him on track when he either wanted to stop or veer off somewhere.

James has absolutely no regrets. Even the things that didn't work out offered an excellent learning process. Sometimes you have to try things out before you can really know whether or not something works for you.

James's future plan is to have significantly increased the income of his property business by the summer of 2015 by switching to cheaper mortgages and paying some of them down to give himself a relatively low loan to value ratio. That will potentially put him in a good position to buy further properties in London when interest rates rise, prices (hopefully) flatten and the market becomes less competitive. Also he intends to start a foundation project shortly for the arts and environment using some of the income from the property business.

Jonathan Stein. Jonathan Stein is a property developer/ trader/investor and portfolio landlord. His property business is involved in property development (refurbishment, conversion, new build), auction trading, title splits and BTL.

He started to invest in 2004. His initial funds were realised by refinancing the flat he was living in in North London. He had inherited some money from his father who had passed away in 2002, but it was not until 2008 that he started to invest on a more aggressive basis. He spent the time between 2004 and 2008 following the market and educating himself. Eventually he gained the confidence to start investing and hasn't looked back since. He has grown his portfolio to over twenty properties through recycling his funds primarily and is now looking to add value to his properties and sell them on for a profit, although he will add to his portfolio again within the next few years.

He wanted to make the transition from his job to being his own boss and take control of his future. He had a long sales and business development career in the corporate world, but never felt that he was financially rewarded properly for his efforts. Since going into property full-time just over eighteen months ago, through auction trading activity, title splits and multi-unit developments he has earned significantly more than he ever did in any year in his corporate career – at least double, and he had a pretty decent salary package.

Jonathan feels it is possible to have money and time in the property business within three years, as outlined in this book. He strongly believes that to get started you will need to self-educate; by this he means keep abreast of all aspects of the property market through the media and attend as many networking events as possible to meet as many people as possible. The more you talk about property the more you will learn and the more ideas you will get. Seeking out a relevant course can be a good idea, but he believes you need to have evaluated all the strategies out there from a top level view to find ones that resonant with you. Then maybe you can choose a relevant course to get a more detailed understanding. Doing it the other way round can be very expensive and overwhelming.

His top tip for beginners starting in property is to network, network, network, at least once a week. His only regret is not realising his potential earlier; he thinks he could have quit his job three to four years before he actually did, but it will always come down to timing and it has to feel right.

His plans going forward are to continue with all the current strategies, but each new development needs to be bigger than the last in terms of the number of units. Within five years he would like to be developing much large properties and sites in excess of fifty units. In addition he is working on the launch of a new web based service for landlords, letting agents and tenants which he hopes will enhance the relationship between landlord and tenant while improving the general image of landlords. Watch this space!

Carly Houston and Kirstin Adam. Carly and Kirstin are sisters. Carly is full-time in the property business, and Kirstin works part-time as an occupational therapist within mental health. They have built a portfolio of HMOs in the Sussex area; as they live in Brighton they wanted all of their properties to be within an hour's drive of where they live.

They specialise in housing local housing allowance (LHA) tenants and they work closely with homeless charities, so all their tenants (with the exception of one professional HMO) have been referred to them by local charities supporting people facing homelessness. They also prioritise tenants with mental health issues; due to Kirstin's background working in mental health this is something they feel passionately about and they are aware that more vulnerable groups may struggle to find long-term accommodation. It was important for them to find a strategy that was in line with their values, contributing positively to their local community and helping more vulnerable social groups. Of course their business has to be profitable, so all of their properties have been purchased using other people's money. They work with investors and Joint Venture (JV) partners so it's important that their properties' cash flows well

Their tenants tend to be 'low priority' in the eyes of the council, which means they have very little chance of getting council housing, so their only option is to rent in the private sector. However many landlords are unwilling to house people claiming benefits. Carly and Kirstin decided to begin working together around two years ago. They had no property investing experience and no money to invest, so they started by educating themselves, buying books and listening to webinars, etcetera. They then started to attend local PIN (property investors network) meetings where they discovered PIN courses, deciding to join Simon Zutshi's year long Property Mastermind Programme in September 2013. They purchased their first property within a few months of starting the course, which really accelerated their business.

Carly was working for a video production company, which was a job she had fallen into rather than something she had chosen. After having had the luxury of being a stay-at-home mum for her two children for around seven years (she had previously worked as a head chef), she realised her family needed her income. Her husband's business was suffering following the economic downturn, but Carly found her job very stressful and felt it was taking her attention away from the kids. She wanted more time and freedom.

Although Kirstin loved her job, it required a long commute. She also found it challenging working for the NHS, seeing jobs and services being cut, and realised that there was no real security or guarantee when it came to her job. When she started thinking about her future she realised that she would need to work full-time until her late sixties with only her NHS pension to look forward to. It was this realisation that prompted Kirstin to explore other options, and property seemed like it could provide an income and security for the family.

The sisters now have a portfolio worth over £2m and an annual net income of around £70k after all the investors have been paid. They have also begun to flip properties which will provide additional income. They feel it's definitely possible to make enough money from property to replace your income and have time within three years. It's not easy, though. It takes commitment, hard work and persistence. It is also really important to get your mindset in the right place as it is very easy to let fear and self-doubt prevent you from taking action. To get started in property, they believe firstly it is really important to educate yourself. There are plenty of resources and courses that are readily available. Do your research to find a course that's right for you.

Their top tip for beginners thinking about starting in property is to work on your mindset. Think about the reason why you want to go into property. If you have a really strong reason why and you emotionalise this it will help you get through the difficult times. Surround yourself with like-minded people and attend networking meetings as these can provide support and inspiration.

Kirstin and Carly have no regrets, just learning, and there has been lots of that. There are things they would do differently in hindsight; there were some decisions they made regarding their refurbishments that have perhaps been more costly than necessary, but overall they are very happy with what they have achieved so far.

Their plan going forward is to continue to work with local housing to house people facing homelessness. They plan to add at least five more HMOs to their existing portfolio this year and to develop their buy to sell model. Kirstin plans to give up her part-time work this year so they will both be full-time in their property business. The next step will be to bring in someone to help with admin and property management to free them both up to spend time with family and pursue things that they enjoy.

Design Your Life

Let me ask you a very honest question: what is your perception of landlords?

Former Labour leader Ed Miliband said, "We need to deal with the terrible insecurity of Britain's private rental market as well. Many tenancies last just six months, with families at risk of being thrown out after that with just two months' notice for no reason", painting landlords in a bad light. As a result Miliband pledged to cap rents and introduce three-year rents in a bid to create stability for landlords and tenants.

In spite of negative media coverage about rich, greedy landlords, an increasing number of UK based landlords are investing in property. Contrary to what Ed Miliband thinks, in my view not all landlords are greedy, mean and evil money making 'what have yous'. I genuinely think that the majority of us invest in property not only for the money, but also for freedom and choice and to get out of the rat race. And we are conscious of the quality of accommodation we provide. The majority of the landlords I have come across provide a good standard of accommodation to their tenants, and in return we get rewarded financially with passive income. That is fair, don't you think?

I genuinely feel that living well is one of the basic entitlements of being human. To me that means having privacy and space, heating, lighting and other mod cons, including a decent kitchen and bathroom with all the required amenities. Above all I like clean houses, and so we provide regular cleaners in all our HMOs. I feel as landlords it is our moral obligation to provide clean living accommodation to all our tenants.

The strategy that worked for me was to convert houses to professional house shares. You need to pick what is right for you using my API method from Section 1.

My question to you, now that you are coming towards the end of this book, is: are you thinking big?

A few months ago my cousin sent me a picture of her twenty-two year old son (my 'nephew') who is working really hard to get a six-pack to get into Bollywood cinema. He wouldn't have dared to dream about it before as it is considered not just difficult but impossible to get cast in a movie without the right connections, but my cousin said that I gave him the inspiration to dream big (aww!).

Just like my nephew, I had a dream of being a Bollywood star. But I didn't dare voice it. And yes, I did crush my own (subconscious) dreams of becoming an actress as I knew I would never have been allowed to have a go at it.

The point I am trying to make is that some of us are too scared of dreaming big dreams. And yes, there is an element of being content with what you have. We should feel thankful and blessed for what we have: our health, our job, having a family, friends; the list can go on. But that should not stop us from chasing our dreams, however big they might be.

To put this into the context of property investing, right now the property market is getting very crowded. One of my goals from 2014 was to expand my knowledge to allow me to invest in larger development deals. One such deal was a plan to convert a large house in North London into six flats and sell it for a profit. We were funding part of the deal by using investor funds and giving them a generous return on their investment; creating a win-win situation is the only way to structure a deal. This project was a steep learning curve for me and I thoroughly enjoyed the experience of working in a consortium of investors and leveraging everyone's strengths.

In the end we lost the deal to a higher bidder, but that did not take away the knowledge I gained in the process. We must not be scared of dreaming big dreams, so make your goals this year big enough to be exciting, challenging and, at times, scary. You have a choice.

You now know that when I started out in 2010 I had little or no experience in property investing. All I had was determination to succeed because of my 'Why', a belief in myself (I have to work on it) and a go-getter attitude. I am truly blessed with a natural dynamic positive energy, but you can create this through the daily disciplines that I have adopted. I used to be a late sleeper and by no means an early riser; motherhood prepared me to change, but you can and must make a conscious effort to follow your dreams. Please read and reread all the tips I have shared in this book. Don't be afraid to dream. We all deserve to live our dream.

I think there is a hero inside each of us. We need to find this hero by searching our souls and asking ourselves what we want to achieve in this lifetime. I would like to share what I personally wanted to achieve with you:

1 To explore the true meaning of life regarding love, peace, truth, happiness and wisdom (knowledge).

2 To enjoy fulfilling relationships with close family members and friends and have loads of fun through enriching experiences (travel the world, theatre, movies, music, shows, dancing; the list is endless).

3 To provide opportunities to my kids and other family members and make a positive difference in their lives and that of the wider community.

Final exercise: Write down your top three life goals.

Summary

The five top reasons why people are not successful in the property business:

1 **Fear.** Fear of making the wrong decision; fear of losing money; fear of letting go of your savings; fear of overspending; fear of over paying for a property; the list is endless. In the property industry we often refer to it as 'False Emotions Appearing Real'.

   To overcome some of these fears always have at least two exit strategies. For example, if you have bought a large house on the assumption that you will get planning permission to convert it into flats but you didn't get the permission, you can add value and sell it on the open market for a profit or rent it as rooms.

   Work positively on your beliefs and mindset. Courage is the antidote to fear. Make courage a habit.

2 **Analysis paralysis.** Depending on the type of personality we have, we can go overboard on the due diligence. Yes it is essential to do your due diligence, but overdo it and you will lose the deal.

   Create a due diligence template spreadsheet for each strategy you are in involved in, for example BTL, HMO, refurbishment or development. If your deal passes the test on the sheet, please make the offer and trust your judgement.

   The due diligence rents, yield and ROI should always be based on worst case scenario.

3 **Risk profile.** A few of us always want to play it safe and consider property too risky. It is only a risk if you are going blindly into the deal. You will not be able to plan for every situation, so be prepared to trust your knowledge and due diligence and take a calculated risk.

4 **Limitations.** We have our self-worth in our mind and subconsciously we programme ourselves to stay within these boundaries. We never give ourselves enough credit for our achievements. Often we have been programmed from childhood to be content; not to be greedy; appreciate what we have. We stop ourselves from thinking bigger thoughts and being more adventurous in our career and business.

A few example of limitations are listed below:
- I am not good enough.
- I don't deserve to be wealthy.
- I'm not special.
- I don't have any talents.

5 **Self-worth and belief.** My childhood was pretty messed up really: no money, no passion, no drive and no direction, although I did have fun. And that theme carried on into my early adult life too. When I was in college I was not committed to doing well academically, although my school results proved I was capable of getting good grades if I put my mind to it. I had a steady relationship (boyfriend) at the time and I was wasting my time thinking about getting married. I didn't have a vision or a dream.

My personal beliefs and mindset. I would like to share with you how some of my personal limitations and beliefs affected how my career took shape.

Growing up in India I was the eldest of four siblings and I was brought up in a traditional conservative Sikh family set up. My dad suffered multiple financial setbacks and the six of us were just about managing in a small one-bedroom flat. To top it all my dad used a small part of the living room as his office. So I grew up believing that I was fated to be poor.

We were always taught that we should be grateful and content with what we had, but secretly I wished I had a better life, my own room, more disposable money. I was always looking at how well my friends lived and was envious of their normal lives. I saw my mum barely managing, and she occasionally had to ask her parents to help out with the finances. It was a terrible mess really.

I think this made me subconsciously think that it was hard to make money and I was not cut out to being rich. I was not worthy. I had the insecure feeling that I must not spend much. In fact, holidays in my early adult life were stressful as I would think I didn't deserve them, blah, blah, blah. There was the fear harking back to my childhood when we didn't have enough and I felt guilty; I should be content and not continue to want more.

I was also very fearful of creditors. Growing up I had issues with people turning up at home and asking for my dad: he owed them money and had been avoiding them, and we had to lie many times and say he was not in the house. To this day when I owe people money I am very conscious of giving it back ASAP.

Next Steps

Ten top tips for your next steps:

1 Work out what you want to achieve.
2 Gain the necessary resources (knowledge and funding in this case).
3 What new rituals and habits do you need? Start writing to-do lists and goals daily.
4 Commit to doing something new every day.
5 Start right now, don't put it off any longer.
6 Get help on your property journey from a coach or mentor.
7 Model other successful investors. Learn from their mistakes.
8 Focus on one or two strategies, avoiding the shiny pennies
9 Keep going; persistence is key.
10 There is no holy grail – the mother of all deals, the 'perfect' deal, doesn't exist.

Top three habits and qualities to be successful:

1 **Perseverance.** Let me be very honest with you and tell you that your property journey will not be easy. You will need to be mentally prepared to suffer setbacks and face challenging situations. You will win deals and clients, lose deals and clients – a mixed bag of positive and negative outcomes.

You will have to motivate yourself every time your plan does not work. And you will be tested, but there is light at the end of the tunnel so you must be persistent.

Managing the deals and funds pipeline in a property business is always every investor's main focus and challenge. You will need to be relentless in looking for the best deals and reliable investors to work with. There have been many times when I have had deals and not the funds, and vice versa. You will need to maintain the right balance between the two and get the timing right.

The first deal can sometimes be the most difficult. Once you've crossed this hurdle it will give you a sense of achievement and the momentum to look for the next deal, and so on and so forth.

2   **Commitment.** How desperately do you need to be financially free? You will need to remind yourself why you embarked on this journey and view your dream chart every day.

3   **Attitude to change.** The economy is influenced by external, political, local and global events. They are out of your control so don't worry about them. Focus on making your business resilient so if you need to change your products and rebrand you can get on with it.

I hit this last challenge as soon as I started my business in 2012. The UK was in recession back then. Property was cheap and it was easy to get deals, but there were not too many investors. Towards the end of 2013 the properly market began to pick up pace, partly due to the economy and partly Government incentives like the Help To Buy Scheme. Bank funding became easier and there was a feel good factor in general.

In 2014 property prices boomed and it was difficult to get deals as estate agents were doing block viewings and sealed bids to push up the prices even more. There were too many investors on the market and not enough deals.

Your business should be able to take the hit and adapt to rapid changes in the market.

My top three habits to help you succeed quicker:

1 **Daily routine.** Creating a morning and evening routine is a must to be successful. My morning routine is a combination of physical and mental exercises to get my body and brain working. I spend an hour doing my daily goals, affirmations, yoga and sit ups.

   My new evening routine is to read for thirty minutes and document my top three goals for the next day.

2 **Follow up.** After every networking event you will need to follow up, ideally within twenty-four hours of the event. This is so your new contacts can remember you. Your network is your net worth, so make an effort to grow your connections and get to know fellow investors. Add their contact details to a spreadsheet and send them an email asking their permission to add them to your database. And very quickly you will go from having tens to hundreds to thousands of connections. Then if you do choose to go full-time into property you can use the database as a potential customer base to give you a kick start.

   Contacting investors over the phone is also a good idea as you can discuss goals and objectives to establish whether there is common ground for you to collaborate and/or help each other.

3   **Abundance mentality.** We must be grateful for what we have, but still have the capacity to dream bigger and believe we deserve better. If we are able bodied, have a roof over our heads and have food on the table we are truly blessed.

Every morning I remind myself of all that I am grateful for. This includes having a healthy, loving, strong, charming and ambitious husband; two healthy children who are bright and beautiful; a loving and compassionate mother; two sisters and a brother who are kind, helpful and generous; two nieces and four nephews who are truly gorgeous; extended family who are helpful and kind; lots of beautiful friends who are caring, forgiving, mature, fun and adventurous. And a lifestyle that allows me to live on my own terms, be my own boss, explore opportunities to grow my business and as a person and have the comforts of a beautiful home, car, housekeeper.

This gratitude allows me to stay grounded. The world looks at us differently if we have an abundance attitude.

My final message to you is that if I can do it, so can you.

Case Study One

The case study below is of a property that I sourced for an investor and converted into a five-bedroom high-end professional HMO.

The property: a mid-terrace four-bedroom house sourced from the open market. The house had been on the market for over six months for £205k. It was generally in a good condition, but needed cosmetic work and an extension to create a living room.

Key features:

1 The ability to create a five-bedroom HMO
2 The ability to force appreciation of the property by adding an extension
3 The property was generally in a good condition

4   A new kitchen had been installed a couple of years ago and was in excellent condition
5   The property had been well looked after by a retired couple
6   The vendors were motivated as they had found a retirement property by the sea and did not want to lose out on that deal
7   One mile away from the town centre/station
8   A five minute bus ride or twenty minutes' walk to town
9   Walking distance from a business park
10 Free parking in the area.

The work required to make it a professional HMO included:

1   Add a shower to the downstairs cloakroom by knocking through the wall to create space
2   Painting, decoration and carpets throughout the property
3   A new extension adjoining the kitchen to create a living room for the professional sharers
4   Fire doors throughout the property, heat detector and smoke alarm.

The extension did not require planning permission because it was within the permitted development. Under the new planning framework you do not need to get planning permission for extensions to homes and business premises, subject to specific limits and conditions. Single-storey rear extension must not extend beyond the rear wall of the original house* by more than three metres on an attached house or four metres on a detached house. For full details visit http://www.planningportal.gov.uk/permission/commonproje cts/extensions/

Below is a copy of the floor plan and pictures of the property before and after the refurbishment.

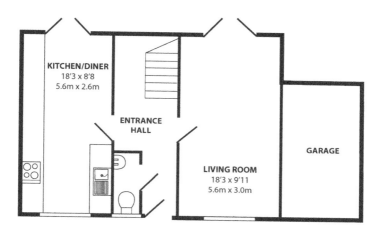

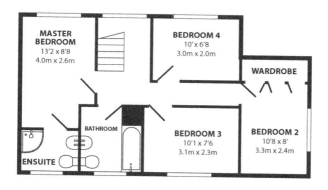

The floor plan after the refurbishment. We added an extension at the back of the kitchen for the communal living room:

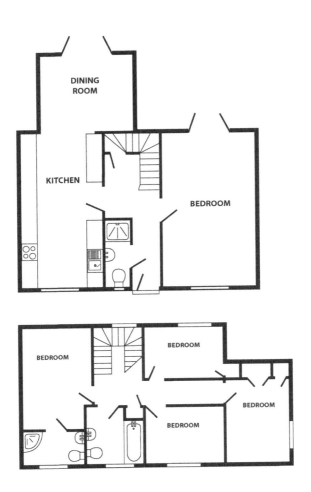

Before and after pictures of the property

Before, cloakroom downstairs.

Work in progress – the picture shows the cloakroom wall being knocked down to create space for a shower

After the shower has been added.

A clear view of the extension boundary from the inside.

Below are professional pictures of the property:

Case Study Two

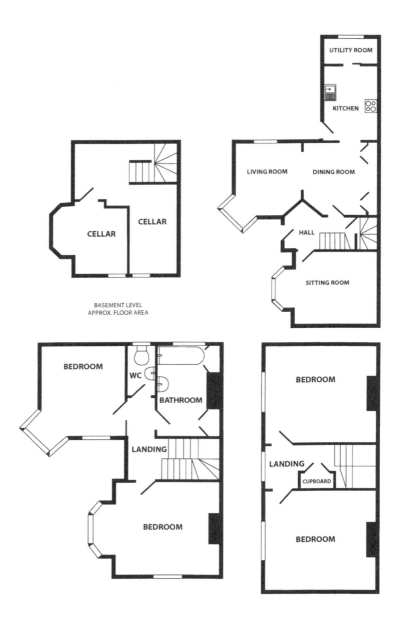

Floor plan above.

The property: A substantial Victorian end of terrace town house within easy reach of Reading town centre. The house offered a luxury kitchen, stripped wood flooring and high ceilings. There were four great sized double bedrooms, two reception rooms and a cellar.

Add value: The plan was to convert it to a six-bedroom high-end professional house share. Externally there was a large garden and we applied for planning permission to build a four-bedroom detached house.

Key features:

1 Semi detached.
2 Corner plot.
3 Four bedrooms.
4 Two reception rooms.
5 Wood flooring luxury kitchen.
6 Garage.
7 Garden cellar.
8 Sash windows.

Issues:

1 The basement could not be used as a bedroom due to ceiling height restrictions.
2 The utility room was damp, had a flat roof and a single skinned extension.
3 Subsidence in the soil caused cracks in 1989 and the property was underpinned in 1990.

4   Insurance companies would not insure it so a structural survey was undertaken by vendor which proved that there had been no subsidence since the underpinning was done.

5   At seven rooms, the planning exercise seemed to be too costly to justify one room over the planning threshold.

6   There was only one bathroom in the house and to achieve premium rents we would need to add en suites to all bedrooms.

Plan of action:

1   Prepare planning application with architect and planning consultant for new build project.

2   Submit planning application on completion of purchase.

3   Give two months' notice to tenants to vacate the property.

4   Refurbishment (approximately six weeks).

5   Submit HMO licence application.

6   Result of planning permission application.

7   HMO readiness.

8   Marketing the property.

9   Tenants check ins.

10 Generate passive income.

Although I am currently waiting for a positive result on the planning permission, the HMO conversion is now complete. See new floor plan and photos below.

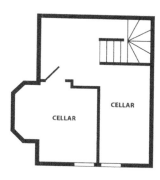

BASEMENT LEVEL

GROUND FLOOR

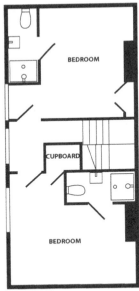

2ND FLOOR

.

Manni, born and brought up in Mumbai, India moved to England when she got married to a British Asian, Romey Chopra. As she was trying to find her feet in the UK, she studied Computers and Business Studies at Brunel University and ended up with a First Class Honours degree.

She landed herself in a good I.T. job (back in the boom times) and moved up the ranks from a Programmer to Project Manager and stayed in corporate for the best part of 12 years.

Over the last 10 years Manni and Romey have built up a personal Property Portfolio worth in excess of £3 million with reasonable equity of around £2 million. The properties are mainly in London and the South East. Their Portfolio is generating a good passive income that supports hers and her family requirements.

During this time she also had two wonderful children, which is when she realised that her life's priorities and perspective had changed. From actually enjoying her job she began to get increasingly frustrated with her job due to lack of time and juggling a challenging job, kids and (a very demanding!) husband.

Manni was adamant that she didn't want to spend the rest of her life in a J.O.B. She was determined to look at alternatives so she could spend quality time with her two children and be there for them.

Manni eventually landed full time in the Property industry in 2012. Manni has not looked back since then and is now financially free and running her own Property business in the South East. She is working hard to build her businesses namely Smart Property Investor (www.smartpropertyinvestor.co.uk) and Investor Lets (www.investorlets.com) and has formulated a niche in acquiring Professional high-end HMOs in Berkshire for herself and other like-minded investors.

Manni Chopra is currently working with a select group of highly experienced and professional investors who invest in small to medium sized development projects. These can range from converting a house to two to three flats and securing sites that have the potential to build new flats and /or houses.

Manni's team at 'Investor Lets' work with investors who want to invest in high-end, high-income generating HMOs in the South East. She offers time-poor Investors the complete armchair HMO Investment service. This consists of finding the right property, managing the refurbishment and also sourcing the right tenants.

Manni has published a book *Property Experts Money Making Secrets* in February 2012 as she is passionate about helping Investors get on to the property ladder. At the time just after the credit crunch period she found that Investors were finding it hard to raise funds and cash flow was low. So she interviewed successful Property Entrepreneurs with tips on how to make £1000 per month while still in a day job. These interviews are published in her book Property Experts Money Making Secrets

Manni's blogs can be found on www.mannichopra.com where you can also download a FREE report on her '5-step tried and tested formula to financial freedom'.

You can also get in touch with Manni by email to manni@mannichopra.com

Lightning Source UK Ltd.
Milton Keynes UK
UKOW07f0758290915

259421UK00012B/67/P